REVIVAL
ON THE HORIZON

12/14/15

Lorallynn
You are very special to me.

YOU ARE
NEEDED TO
A IGNITE
REVIVAL

RUTH JOHNSON
WITH BARRY JOHNSON

REVIVAL ON THE HORIZON
First Edition November 2015

ISBN: 978-0-9661470-3-2
Library of Congress Catalog Card Number: 2015956395
Copyright © 2015 Lighthouse of Hope Publications

Published by:
Lighthouse of Hope Publications
PMB #365
914 164th Street S.E. #B-12
Mill Creek, Washington, U.S.A. 98012-6339

Printed in the United States of America

ACKNOWLEDGEMENTS

Pastor Doug Martin
Associate Pastor, our Home Church, Sonrise Christian Center, Everett WA
Pastor Doug is a very special man whom my husband, Barry and I greatly respect and deeply appreciate as both our pastor and our friend. He also inspired several important improvements in the final writing of key places in this book. I am immensely grateful for his precise, incredibly insightful wisdom so that the message of "Revival on the Horizon" could become as effective and as clear as possible.

Pastor Hughes Protzman
Associate Pastor, Mukilteo Foursquare Church, Mukilteo WA
Pastor Hughes has been an ongoing source of encouragement to Barry and me for many years. His understanding of the message that burns in our hearts and his believing in what we are called to impart to the Body of Christ have often given us renewed courage to keep pressing on. We both are immensely thankful for this dedicated pastor who exemplifies in every way a loving, kind, caring shepherd after God's own heart.

Pastor John Gravallese
Former Senior Pastor, Hosanna Christian Fellowship
Currently Way of Holiness Prison Ministry
One morning when I had just begun to write "Revival on the Horizon," Pastor John began to pour out his heart to me about how strong the presence of God is on each of my books and how they always cause him to weep. He had no idea I was struggling with wondering about the value of writing another book. So his timely encouragement significantly helped me to believe that God could touch people's lives through what was burning in my spirit to express in "Revival on the Horizon." Therefore I'm overwhelmingly thankful for how the Father used Pastor John at the very moment in my life when I seriously needed the words he spoke to me.

Ashley Shepherd
A young person age 30, Germantown, Maryland

Ashley wrote to my husband, Barry and I regarding us having an impact on the younger generation in the new season we are entering into in this ministry. What's amazing is that we've never met this precious young person and this is how she described she knew me:

> *"Today I was looking through my stack of teaching notes and words from the days of revival during my early adolescence into young adulthood. It was a time when I searched for anything and everything to sustain me. That is when I came across a prophetic word that you wrote, Ruth in 2002. I had printed it out and marked it up at that time. I was very young when I first found it, around seventeen or eighteen. Yet as I read it today, the words you prophesied ring true and speak volumes into where I am right now. They have birthed hope in me again."*

At that time Ashley had no idea I had just started to write a book that Barry and I passionately wanted God to use to stir up hope and a renewed sense of meaningful purpose in young people. So God bless you, Ashley. The Father used you in an incredible way to encourage me just when I began trying to put into words what He wanted captured in "Revival on the Horizon."

Pastor Denny Finnegan
Interim Pastor, Bethel Evangelical Presbyterian Church, Enon Valley, PA

Pastor Finnegan's insights that he sent me after he reviewed "Revival on the Horizon" were a tremendous help in the development of several of the chapters. The investment of his time and effort to help in this way is truly appreciated.

Koenn Becker
An amazing Freshman in High School, Bothell, WA

Koenn's passion for the message in "Revival on the Horizon" reaching people, especially the younger generation, exploded into the design of his remarkable Cover. I'm so grateful for how God used this special young man to capture the fire and hope for Revival that is at the very heart of this book.

WHAT OTHERS ARE SAYING

"After many boxes of Kleenex and praise times of thanks, I was able to conclude the reading of 'Revival on the Horizon.' I so enjoyed Ruth's openness and truth. Such a story of what seemed like great tragedy, to the ultimate triumph. What Ruth has described in this book is love in action. How to forgive. How to receive. How to give the love of God. I want to thank Ruth and Barry for doing this great work for the Lord. So many times we tell the old, old stories and how great they are. But every now and then there is a new story and how great it is to tell it abroad. I believe that although the church has a wonderful history, the half has not yet been told. It is time for the church to be the story again and leave more new history. Let's continue, as Ruth and Barry have demonstrated, and put our love in action. There is a Revival on the horizon and the horizon is visible. For those who have eyes to see, it is here. I pray this book will be a best seller. Such truth is seldom told. But here it is!"

Pastor Edwin Wile

Church Planter, Retired Pastor, Gateway Worship Center, Gravenhurst, Ontario Canada

"The more our culture turns against Christianity, the more we need to heed the message of this book because it's the only way that hearts will be opened to receive Jesus. In our church we are starting a new ministry in a large apartment complex and we're going to apply the principles of this book to this new ministry. I believe we'll see people receive Jesus and families will be healed. They will walk out of darkness and begin to walk in the light. Thank you for this timely message."

Pastor Hughes Protzman

Associate Pastor, Mukilteo Foursquare Church, Mukilteo, WA

"'Revival on the Horizon' is a must read for this generation! God's heart for revival to be ignited and set ablaze in this day and in this generation is vital for the release and establishment of His purposes for all His sons and daughters. In this book, Ruth vulnerably shares her heart and powerfully integrates the Word of God to point to the absolute need for love and freedom to be the catalyst that put us on the path to revival. It's not out of reach. It's the heart, plan and desire of the Father. A genuine love is poured out through these pages as Ruth and Barry share testimonies of redemption and transformed lives, offering hope and encouragement to every reader."

Pastors Russ and Kim Babcock

Missions and Family Life Pastors at The Pursuit NW Church, Snohomish, WA, Hospitality Directors for "Marked By Heaven," a Ministry in Guadalajara, Mexico that is sacrificially making a radical difference for Orphans in Latin America.

"Ruth writes with a striking compassion for the church, for young people, and for those who have been broken in life so that they can find hope in God and unity with God's family, the church. These pages are filled with hope and encouragement that He can truly change your life."

Pastor John Hammer

Senior Associate Pastor, our Home Church, Sonrise Christian Center, Everett, WA

"This is an excellent book. It is transparent. People can identify with the events of Ruth and Barry's lives that they have shared and this is very important. They have not only shared their stories, but also they've given direction, answers and hope. These are the things that people need. I believe this book will be a great source of freedom and hope for many people."

Pastor Doug Martin

Associate Pastor, our Home Church, Sonrise Christian Center, Everett, WA

"Ruth and Barry have a powerful testimony and teaching about how to let God's forgiveness minister to us and through us to others. I thank them for asking me to be a part of this prophetic work! I truly believe that this book offers you and me the possibility of moving forward in our sufferings through forgiveness so that we might bring to others the comfort of Christ in the same way that He has given it to us."

Pastor Denny Finnegan
Interim Pastor, Bethel Evangelical Presbyterian Church, Enon Valley, PA

"In this book, Ruth touches on topics that are very real and that people grapple with in their daily lives. She writes about questions that don't always have simple answers, such as: How can God, who holds control in all things, allow suffering and pain in the lives of His children? That is a very real issue everyone can relate to at some point in their lives. My hope and prayer is that this book will find its way into many hands and its truths will be a catalyst for the Holy Spirit to set people free from the limitations they have lived under. As a result of reading Ruth's book, I also pray that many will spread their eagle wings and forever 'fly the coop' to soar as they were meant to. Ruth's heart of compassionate love for God's people comes through on every page. You will be encouraged and strengthened as you read it!"

Diane Fink
Speaker, Author, Edmonds, WA

"Ruth and Barry truly live what they preach. They have 'shaken off' the things that held them back and are living in Revival. The message in this book will cause you to 'rise up like an Eagle.' Reading it will stir a longing in your heart to be all that God wants you to be. You'll be so encouraged. You'll be able to believe there is still hope."

Britt Danley
Speaker, Shoreline, WA

"Ruth's book shines like a beacon of hope for Revival, both personal and corporate. Within its pages the heartbeat of God can be heard. Had I read this book months earlier, I would have had no need of months of counseling because it tore open places in my heart and filled them with healing and hope. I was also moved to tears as I read Ruth and Barry's testimonies. Truly the hand print of God is stamped upon this book!"

Linda McManness

"Songs of the Potter Ministry" to Israel, Cincinnati, Ohio.

"'Revival on the Horizon' is a beautiful depiction of the greatest love story told by a woman with a relentless passion to see it lived out in the hearts of the believer in order to reach a lost and fatherless generation. I feel that the message and heartbeat of this book will be instrumental to the radical awakening of this younger generation and the generations to come. It is also my heartfelt belief that there is going to be a mighty impartation of inheritance through Ruth and Barry to this generation and a bringing forth of new life to those of us, who like me, once tasted and saw the glory of the Lord. But we've been derailed and are left longing to see it again, afresh and anew."

Ashley Shepherd

A young person age 30, Germantown, Maryland

"This is a generation where so many of us are without fathers and mothers who loved and protected us. Yet in this book we encounter a Father who will never let us down. Our generation was also taught that unless we do something 'big,' we are not important and the sooner we do that "big" thing, the more important we will be. But if this does not happen by the time we reach our early to mid-twenties, we have failed. We have missed our chance. This book makes it so clear that this isn't the truth at all. I feel wholeheartedly that 'Revival on the Horizon' will touch the lives of all who read it, including the younger generation. But especially those who are lost, hurting and longing for purpose in their lives. That's what happened to me. I discovered a renewed sense of hope and purpose as I read it."

Julie Dougherty

A young person age 30, Everett, WA

"There is a serious need for a Revival today like the one that shook the nations in the Book of Acts. That's why this book is exactly what is needed because it captures the choices that make it possible for Revival to take place and it describes the ones that can kill even the hope of it happening. It's also painful to know that many of the feelings and hurts in this book are what my generation is going through and they don't know how to deal with it. So I appreciate that Ruth really has a heart for young people and she wants to give them hope. She also relates to the hurts that people face because she's been there herself. This makes what she writes even more powerful."
Koenn Becker
A remarkable young person in High School, Bothell, WA

"'Revival on the Horizon" talks about how desperately my generation needs to be loved. Young people are hurting everywhere I go and I can see that this love is needed. That's why this book is so important. It will help my generation who are hurting more than ever before to find that love."
Aaron Becker
An amazing young man at age 16, Bothell, WA

DEDICATION

My husband Barry

Ever since Barry and I were married in 1991, he has encouraged me to be everything I was created by God to be. It is his kind, never changing support that has kept me going during the hard times in fulfilling my calling and it means everything to me that we walk closely together as a husband and wife team in ministry. I am also deeply moved by the strong mantle on Barry as a "father in the faith" each time I witness God using him to reach into the hearts of the younger, hurting generation who often have never known a father's love. Then on a daily basis I get to personally see how sincerely Barry lives everything he teaches. This is why whatever he imparts to the Body of Christ comes from an integrity that I immensely respect. Therefore it's an honor to dedicate "Revival on the Horizon" to such a special man, my best friend and the greatest inspiration in my life.

Matthew, Koenn, Aaron Becker

It is my great joy to also dedicate this book to these three young men who at the time it was being written were twelve, fourteen and sixteen. I met weekly with them over many months while they described to me how young people are suffering. I often experienced tears. Then new parts of "Revival on the Horizon" were birthed that became a critical part of it reaching across the generations to affect all ages, including youth who are seriously in need of encouragement and hope. I will never forget those months with Matthew, Koenn and Aaron when they shared their hearts and lives with me in such an unforgettable way. All of my days I will remember that we experienced those amazing times together.

THE CHAPTERS

Chapter One

RADICAL LOVE

To be loved is the deepest longing of the human heart. The longer anyone lives without it, the more painful their loneliness and emptiness will become. Yet when people encounter sincere caring, a miracle can happen that can change them. It can renew their courage to not give up on the Father using them. It can restore their hope and give those who are already grappling with despair a reason to want to live.

This is a true account of a man from a remote mountain in East Africa who was in despair because this love was missing in his life. He is a pastor who came into our lives when my husband, Barry and I lived in Uganda and gathered strategic leaders from across that nation to live in tents on our compound. They came from tribes that violently hated each other.

We taught them this message about love and then helped them to personally experience it. One of these leaders was a pastor from Mt. Elgon and he told us this gripping testimony:

> "In my village and in my church you can sit next to someone and it's as if they are 10,000 miles away from you. Even if you've known them for many years, there's no closeness and when they speak to you, their words are tough and harsh. Love doesn't exist on the Mountain and many people want to die. They have so many problems, but no one cares. No one loves them. They hate themselves.

They feel such hopelessness that it's very common to walk along a path deep in the villages and find dead men who have hung themselves by the neck on a tree because they couldn't live another day without someone loving them.

I'm one of those men.

I came here wanting to die. I planned on killing myself when I went home after this seminar. I couldn't stand feeling so completely alone in my troubles anymore. I even decided I wouldn't come here with an open heart.

Yet when I came here to Ruth and Barry's Village Compound, everyone immediately is the Family of God. It's like we've known one another all of our lives. This I've never seen before. But when I saw how everyone changed while we listened to Ruth and Barry teach about love and unity, I also changed. I became full of joy and now I'm different. I want to live! And when I go back, I'm bringing this new love to my family. Then I will bring it to the hopeless all over the Mountain!"

We traveled to Mt Elgon a month later and searched for this man everywhere we went. One night it happened. When we arrived at a remote church, he stepped out of the shadows to greet me. I cried tears of joy as I asked him, "How are you? I wanted so much to see you and know that you are alright."

"My whole life has changed," he responded, his eyes ablaze with a vibrant joy. "Everything is different now. I'm kind to my family. I'm also telling people about this love I learned. I returned to the Mountain with a reason to live!"

It's tragic that across the generations, tribes, cultures and nations, more and more of God's own children are feeling empty inside, just like that man from the Mountain.

They long for a sense of community.

They need a place where they belong, where someone "sees" them and cares about them.

Many no longer find this at church, even though Jesus came so that a closeness based on caring love could happen for us in the Body of Christ. This loss can hurt so much that sincere, good hearted Christians are deciding to not get involved in a church anymore.

But disconnecting is *not* the answer.

It only increases the isolation. It causes people to feel even more desperately alone. Therefore what's needed is believers "seeing" those passing by us each day whom the Father longs for us to care about for Him, including at church.

And those people are...

Young and old who are feeling heartache and distress in their relationships and they can't find any way to be at peace.

Children who are consumed with fear. They feel like their lives are being ripped apart because Mom and Dad are fighting.

Single mothers who go to bed each night hurting for their kids. They wish they could take away their pain. But they know they can't.

Those who don't see any way out of their regrets. They are tormented because of the guilt they feel about mistakes in their past that it's impossible to go back and do differently.

There are those passing by us each day, including when we are at church, who feel that life can never get better for them and they need to be encouraged. But those around them are oblivious to what they are up against and how great their ache is for someone to see them and care. These lovers of Jesus have no one to be there for them. They are walking through their days, and living their nights, completely alone. Many have sunk into hopelessness. They've given up. They are drowning in despair.

Then there are so many young people who are hurting in ways that are far worse than any previous generation. Digital abuse from social media through "cyber bullying" is having a devastating impact by telling them: "You'll never amount to anything. So why bother trying. You should just give up and end your life."

This is a deadly message for those who are already struggling with thoughts of giving up. Tragically, some young do believe it and kill themselves.

There are youth being bombarded in their most vulnerable places where they are still innocent and unprepared.

It's coming from sexual predators, pornography, people with wrong intentions trying to have access to them through the Internet, and many other ways.

They are being mentally and emotionally battered by disturbing videos of the worst things happening in the world that frequently have horrific, graphic details.

Others are living in neighborhoods that are a nightmare. Gangs, drugs, violence, and dangers to them even staying alive are a way of life for them. Their frightening world hardens and defeats them when they are still just a little boy or a very young, little girl. They are drowning in so much pain that before they ever have a chance to hang on to any hope for the future at all, it is killed while they are still a child. The comradery of the gangs gives them a place they feel they can belong somewhere, and to someone.

Youth being devastated in any of these ways scars their hearts.

It cripples their future.

What makes all this horribly worse is so many have grown up without love or any help from a father, Many have never experienced the steadying comfort of a mother. They feel there's no one who is even aware of what they are going through because they have no one who cares. As a result of this overwhelming load of frightening, heartbreaking feelings, there are more suicides among young people today than we've ever seen.

I once was one of those lost, hurting youth.

My family lived in the Projects. I have vivid memories of what a scary, treacherous place it is to grow up. Every day I felt that my life could be violently ended. I was too terrified to ever just walk home from school. I always ran as fast as I could so that I could escape getting beat up again by one of the gangs that waited every day to pounce on me.

Throughout each night, I couldn't sleep because of frantic screams, sirens, gun shots and screeching cars outside my bedroom window.

At the same time, I never had a safe mother or father.

I was experiencing the worst kinds of abuse in our home. Four of us kids, at different moments, were screaming from what was being done to us. Hearing what was happening to my younger brother and older sister is what hurt me the most. I was horribly troubled that I was so helpless to stop the terrible things being done to them.

In the midst of this much darkness, peace was not possible.

Life was only a treacherous ordeal of survival. I felt lost and empty, with no way out of the pain I constantly was drowning in.

It could have changed my life if someone had seen me and tried to encourage me when I was one of those troubled young people.

Finally, passing by us whom we need to see are those in the Body of Christ in their late twenties and early thirties who were passionately in love with Jesus when they were younger.

They had dreamed about making a radical difference in this world and being used mightily in ministry. But hard times and the harsh realities and responsibilities of life have turned those hopes and dreams into disillusionment. What they had believed about God's destiny for them hasn't worked out the way they thought it would at all.

RADICAL LOVE

Consequently, more and more of the younger generation are giving up on any hope of the Father's plan for them happening. To help them find new courage and revived hope in how the Father sees them they need kind "mothers and fathers in the faith" in the Family of God who notice them, care about them, and speak words of life to them.

What's extraordinary to me is how much Jesus actually lived like this. He didn't just walk by people as if they didn't exist or they weren't worth taking up His time. He saw them.

And yes, He went to the multitudes. But He spent most of His time reaching out with love to one or two people at a time.

It's also remarkable that they were simple, ordinary, seemingly unimportant people He gave His time to.

When living like that becomes our own passion, then we can walk in the footsteps of Jesus. We can have the same miraculous impact on people that He did. This is a story of what it looked like after the Awakening to that kind of love happened to me.

It was Easter Sunday in Africa. We were excitedly looking forward to ministering in Kampala. The pastor has reserved a beautiful room. But when we arrived it was and the only room available to meet in was a raunchy bar.

The pastor and his wife were horrified that this was the place we would be on Easter Morning. As we walked in, it was ominously dark. Gaudy beer signs covered the walls and the dirt floor reeked with the nauseating smell of vomit, old urine and fecal matter. Rough looking men lurked in the shadows, drinking heavily and talking crudely. Several youth were playing a game of pool and looked up menacingly at us as we walked in. Young, scared girls were waiting to make money by letting men doing whatever they wanted to them. It hurt to see the hopelessness and fear in their eyes.

"What's God going to do?" Barry and I silently wondered.

When the service started, I immediately launched into this story:

> "Jesus was born in a humble stable with the smells and filth of animals all around Him. He could have chosen a fancy palace to be born in.
>
> But He didn't.
>
> He chose a place that was lowly, just like this run down bar. He also was criticized for spending time with the prostitutes and sinners. Yet He went to those who knew they were lost and brought the kind love of His Father to them."

One of the prostitutes began to sob.

Many were so affected by her weeping that they also began to cry as I continued to talk.

"Because Jesus came for the simple and humble, He's very happy all of us are here. And to honor Him this Easter morning, we are going to bow down and worship Him."

At that point most of the men glared at me, as if to say, "Yeah right, lady."

They were shocked when I invited everyone to gather in a circle on the filth encrusted floor.

Yet when they came, a miracle happened. At the first sound of our worship with the harp, heaven descended and everyone suddenly fell to their knees. Many wept and bowed low before God as the visitation of His presence enveloped them. Soon not one person was still standing. What made this miraculous is that only the pastors and our Team were saved.

The service ended a short time later due to it being swelteringly hot under a low-pitched roof made of metal sheeting as the temperature rose to a hundred and ten degrees. I sensed that the Father wanted me to go to the teens who were playing pool. Amazingly, when I walked up to them, they respectfully stopped their game.

"Thank you for trying so hard not to make much noise during our service," I told them. "I want you to know I appreciate it. May I give you a hug?"

I opened my arms wide and one by one they came over to me and welcomed me hugging them and holding them, as if they were my own sons.

Tears welled up in their eyes and their faces softened while they told me, "What you were doing and saying really affected us."

Moments later we said goodbye. As we walked to our van, a young African on our team explained to me:

"Those are the worst kind of troublemakers here in Kampala. It's shocking that they were so affected by what took place and that they talked to you like that.

This was a miracle. Everything that happened was a miracle. There's no way those boys or the prostitutes would go to church this morning.

So God came to them!"

Two weeks went by and we heard a knock on our gate. The pastor over the Easter service had just arrived to excitedly tell us:

"After you left that Sunday the prostitutes asked my wife and me how they could be born again and we led them to the Lord. Then from the time you were there, the owner feared to use that building for a bar because he said on Easter 'God came.'

So he turned it over to me and told me that now it can only be used as a church.

Already we are growing. New people are coming in.

The owner even comes to our church with his wife."

I will never forget the faces of those tough looking teens and the scared, young girls, and how much simple expressions of kindness affected them.

Yet God can use **any** child of His to have that impact on another life. The problem is that those fleeting encounters can easily seem like they are "no big deal," though the truth is they can change someone's life.

These are examples in the ministry of Jesus of those kinds of brief, but powerful moments:

There was a man in a tree who was invisible to the crowd. Yet Jesus saw him and in the midst of a crowd He cared about him. Demonstrating that He genuinely cared about this one man was important to Jesus.

Then there was a woman who had been suffering for many years with bleeding. She was desperate to just get near Jesus and be comforted and helped. In the midst of all those people pressing in on Him, Jesus saw her. He was deeply moved with compassion by her suffering. He cared about this one, troubled soul as if she were at that moment the only person in the crowd.

On another day He encountered a leper who was a despised, untouchable outcast. He was cruelly shunned and sadly watched others experiencing life, while never being a part of it.

But Jesus was different. His heart was moved with compassion by this leper's suffering. He included this "outsider" in His amazing love. He reached out to this outcast with sincere kindness.

There was also a distressed woman. Others could only see her failures. Yet Jesus looked beyond her glaringly obvious mistakes and saw her heart. He didn't condemn her for her wrong choices. His nonjudgmental love ignited a transformation in her. It set her heart free.

As I've been on this Journey of learning how to love, I was really surprised when I first saw that Jesus wasn't super spiritual or preachy about doing this. Whatever He said to express caring to people came from His heart and in the most simple, humble ways. There was never anything fancy or grand about His words. For example, when Lazarus died He hardly said anything at all. Instead He unashamedly wept the tears of someone who was sincerely affected by seeing the grief of those who had lost a brother. This is what those moments looked like.

"Mary went to the place where Jesus was. When she saw Him, she fell at His feet and said, 'Lord, if You had been here, my brother would not have died.' When Jesus saw Mary crying and the Jews who came with her also crying, He was upset. He was deeply troubled. He asked, 'Where did you bury him?' 'Come and see, Lord,' they said. Jesus cried. So the Jews said, 'See how much He loved him.'"

John 11:32-36 NCV

How amazing that He didn't tell those grieving what a great thing it was that their loved one was in heaven.

He didn't even quote a scripture to give them something positive to think about.

He also didn't say any of these preachy, spiritually sounding words that so often Christians say to those who are having a hard time:

Be at peace.
God is in control.

Don't fear.
It's all in God's hands.

Don't be anxious.
God will work this for good.

Keep your eyes on God.
He won't let you down.

Trust God.
It's all in His hands.

Jesus **never** talked to anyone who was hurting in this preachy, super spiritual way.

He only expressed in the simplest ways how much He genuinely identified with their grief and suffering. Then through living that way He showed us that **this** is how to react to people when they are dealing with any kind of overwhelming loss:

"Be happy with those who are happy.

Be **sad** with those who are sad."
Romans 12:15 NCV

Ever since Jesus returned to His Father over 2000 years ago, Christians with the best of intentions have collected ways of relating to people that are not how He would treat them. For example, those in the Body of Christ who are grieving over the death of a loved one or are up against another kind of catastrophic loss are often getting terribly hurt when they are among believers.

Sometimes being at church can be one of the **most** painful places to be if you are going through a really hard time. This is a description of what can cause that hurtfulness, even when people are only trying to be sincerely caring:

Christians minimizing someone's heartache and loss.

Ignoring their pain, as if it's not happening and changing the subject to something more cheery and uplifting.

Skipping over the person's tears and heartache and jumping to statements of victory.

Giving suggestions about what the person can do to help themselves feel better, such as health, exercise or nutrition ideas.

Going preachy on them, as if to say that their grief and tears need to be fixed with a really spiritual solution.

Jesus showed us by His humble, sincere example that a grieving person needs someone to be kind and caring to them, right where they are. But for this to become the way we express love, we need to learn how to make what matters the most to the Father, what is the most important to us.

These are glimpses into what His "most important things" look like:

Jesus was asked, "What is the most important commandment in the law of Moses?" He replied: "You must love the Lord your God with all your heart, all your soul, and all your mind. This is the first and the greatest commandment.

A second is **equally** important. Love your neighbor as yourself. All the other commandments and all the demands of the prophets are based on these two commandments."

Matthew 22:36-37 NLT

"I was hungry, and you gave Me food. I was thirsty, and you gave Me something to drink. I was alone and away from home, and you invited Me into your house. I was without clothes, and you gave Me something to wear. I was sick, and you cared for Me. I was in prison, and you visited Me."

Then the good people will answer, "Lord, when did we see You hungry and give You food, or thirsty and give You something to drink? When did we see You alone and away from home and invite You into our house? When did we see You without clothes and give You something to wear? When did we see You sick or in prison and care for You?"

The King will answer: "I tell you the truth, anything you did for even the least of My people, you also did it for Me.'"

Matthew 25: 35-40 NCV

"What a wonderful God we have. He is the Father of our Lord, Jesus Christ, the source of every mercy and the one who so wonderfully comforts and strengthens us in our hardships and trials. And why does He do this? So that when others are troubled and they need our compassion and encouragement, we can pass on to them this same help and comfort God has given us."

2 Corinthians 1:3-4 TLB

"God sets the lonely in families. He is a Father to the fatherless and a defender of widows. Pure and genuine religion in the sight of God the Father means caring for orphans and widows in their distress and refusing to let the world corrupt you."

Psalm 68:5-6 NIV, James 1:27 NLT

The genuine caring that is captured in those descriptions of what God's love looks like is how the early believers actually lived.

Then it was their clearly demonstrated love that set the world on fire in the Book of Acts. It was also such a genuinely kind way of treating each other that it drew the unsaved into the church as they witnessed something they'd never seen before. And from those who had been radically changed by loving this way came the astoundingly powerful miracles that a hurting, lost world desperately needed.

But eventually that fire went out.

Since the death of that Revival, there's been an ache in God's heart for the same love His Son gave His all to impart would be restored to His church.

At times down through the ages this has begun to happen when there was an explosion of signs and wonders and miracles that ignited a powerful move of God. But those miraculous manifestations have never been enough for any Revival to continue and spread.

My husband, Barry captures why:

> "Jesus knew that without love and unity, the impact of the miraculous would be short lived.
>
> Look at His ministry.
>
> He healed, fed and set many free from demons. Yet most of these same people deserted Him.
>
> So although He had a miraculous ministry, He was very aware that the miraculous alone would not turn the world upside down. That could only happen when a united group of believers finally understood what it meant to love one another and to worship and pray with a unity that was based on that love.
>
> Sure the miracles, signs and wonders after Pentecost had an impact on the unsaved.
>
> But what ignited in the Book of Acts Revival and caused it to spread was a raging blaze of unprecedented love that changed the world. In approximately ten years, this Revival Fire was seen throughout the Roman Empire.
>
> It became the most spectacular one in history."

> *Barry Johnson*

Now is an urgent time for this Jesus kind of love to be ignited again and spread like wildfire in this generation.

Yet for this to become possible, those who know Him need to find their way back to genuinely living the caring about people that He sacrificed His life to teach us.

Without this love being restored to the church, Christianity becomes empty to the saved and meaningless to the world.

This is why Jesus said:

"As you have heard from the beginning, My command is for you to live this life of love. For those who do not love their brothers and sisters are not My Father's children and whoever does not love, does not know Him, because He is love." Jesus

2 John NCV, I John 3:10, 4:8 NCV
Personalized

One of the believers who caught that fire was Peter. From the moment he began to follow Jesus, he watched this unusually special Man react to different situations. He personally saw what was important to Jesus. Then gradually, through shared experiences, a powerful bond was forged. Peter described one of those unforgettable moments when he wrote toward the end of his life:

RADICAL LOVE

"We ourselves heard the voice when we were
there with Him on the Holy Mountain."
2 Peter 1:18 NLT

Peter also watched what hurt his Friend.

He surely could never forget the heartrending pain in Jesus' eyes when he betrayed the love of the one Person who had never given up on him, despite him making so many mistakes and having so many mixed up ideas about what being a follower of Jesus was all about.

He knew the others would never have allowed him to continue walking closely with Jesus in His ministry. They had seen all his "mess ups." So they easily could have decided he was not good enough to be used by God in any "important" ways at all.

But Jesus looked past all of Peter's failures.

He saw his sincere, special heart and loved him, no matter what. Jesus believed in him. He knew that Peter's humble brokenness is always what means the most to His Father when He wants to use someone to make a difference in the lives of others.

Nonetheless, all Peter could see was how he had terribly failed. His devastation over betraying such a rare, unconditional, forgiving love is captured in these wrenching words:

"At that moment
the Lord turned and looked at Peter.
Then Peter remembered and he broke down and cried."
Mark 14:72 NLT, Luke 22:61 NLT

This actually means in the original language that he sobbed uncontrollably. He was so heartbroken that he had failed his Friend, he was never the same. For the rest of his life, he loved Jesus with a magnitude of devotion that is born from the agony of letting someone down who had only been fiercely, loyally good to him.

It was a depth of relationship that came from him experiencing that Jesus loved him so much, He completely forgave Peter's betrayal and remembered it no more. Whenever this rare kind of love happens to anyone, it leaves an unforgettable imprint on the heart. Peter was so affected that what mattered the most to Jesus became part of him. For example, he never forgot that the Lord said, "All people will know that you are My followers if you love each other." John 13:34-35 NCV Then in his final writings, Peter penned these passionate, deeply moving words:

> "See to it that you really do love each other ***intensely*** and with ***all*** your hearts. I will keep on reminding you of these things as long as I live. I want you to remember them long after I am gone."
>
> 1 Peter 1:22 NLT, 2 Peter 1:12-15 NLT

This same Jesus who changed the course of Peter's life found me in 1973.

I was only thirty years old.

But I had already given up on wanting to live. A long time before Jesus found me, I had buckled under the crushing weight of my devastating losses.

I no longer had the courage to dream, though from a young age I had a longing to serve God. The last flicker of hope had died in my soul.

Trapped in the deadly abyss of bitter hatred, I was drowning in a frightening despair. I couldn't see any way out of the scary darkness as terrorizing fear paralyzed me.

I was so young.

Yet haunting regrets tormented me day and night.

I didn't think I could ever stop feeling so desperately alone.

Every day I thought about how to kill myself to end the pain.

I ached for just one person to see me, and care.

Then just like what happened to Peter, a whole new world suddenly opened up to me when Jesus found me. I was loved for the first time in my life and He immediately began to tenderly reassure me with what He says to every child of God:

**"You never have to face life alone again.
Now, I'm always with you."**

For the first time, laughter bubbled up from the core of my being and God's presence beamed from my smile.

Then somewhere along the way, the message that means so much to my Friend became my own. I passionately wanted to spend the rest of my life imparting it to others.

Though decades have gone by since all this began for me, I feel even more strongly the Father's grief that the kind of love His Son paid such a horrific price to teach us has grown cold among many of His own children.

This loss is tragic because it's happening at a time when great darkness is increasing upon the nations of the earth. Consequently, there's an even more desperate need for God's children to find their way back to the kind of love that Jesus came to help us understand.

That's why at this time in the history of Christianity, the Father is imploring us:

"Please remember, as if it was only yesterday, why My Son Jesus came.

Please don't let the remembrance of Him grow dim for you with the passage of time. I beg of you to be moved by this plea from My heart.

Though the whole world may forget how My Son lived, and why He died, please don't forget that He came to show you how to take My love to a hurting, lost world that is in so much pain, and suffering with darkness and hopelessness.

These are the ones passing by you each day who are in great need of experiencing through you the simple, humble kindness of My love.

Please carry an awareness of all this in your heart wherever you go.

Then even without a word being spoken, you will carry My presence. Then as you pass through the marketplace where people reject Me and despise Me, wondrous things will happen, just like happened to My friend Peter.

That is how close I yearn for you to walk with Me at a time when the embers of the Gospel have grown cold, even among many of My own children.

I plead with you in the days ahead hear the cries of My heart for the discouraged and those in distress who have no peace.

They are lost.

They don't know how to find My hope.

As never before, please long to have the love I revealed through My Son Jesus burn in your being like fire so that you can bring it to them for Me.

While you take all this into your heart, I promise that I will use you in ways to make a difference in the lives of countless people in your lifetime, and most often one life, one moment at a time, just like what happened to My Son."

- Your Father and your Dad

Chapter Two

REVIVAL ON THE HORIZON

Revival is not about a new truth being revealed.

It's always the restoration of a lost truth that the Father longs for His people to earnestly care about once again.

This is why there is a desperate need in this hour for an Awakening to the truths of love and unity that in the early church "turned the world upside down." Acts 17:6 AMP

That taking place drew in the unsaved as they witnessed a genuine love and an unselfish unity between the new believers that they had never seen before. Then down through the ages, the story of God's people has been about the ache in the Father's heart for these radically life-changing truths to be restored to His church.

What is sad is that multitudes of believers no longer even know what Word-based unity looks like.

Yet when "being of one heart and one mind and one spirit" becomes only a distant memory of something amazing that happened a long time ago, then much of what Jesus suffered and died to give us also becomes more distant, even irrelevant to God's own children.

The challenge is that human nature wants to have its own way.

Therefore when Christians feel they have a right to do their own thing in a body of believers, they will often speak against and judge any leader who doesn't allow them to do whatever they want.

However this Biblically disloyal, negative talk causes division and when unity is lost, love dies.

The challenge is that it's not easy to live the way Jesus talked about. It requires that we face anything we are personally doing that's hurting relationships within the church. We also have to be willing to lay down, at times, what we want in order for the unselfishness of unity to be possible. This is a powerful picture of what that looked like in the Book of Acts:

"*All* the believers were united
as they lifted their voices in prayer.

After this prayer, the building where they were meeting
shook and they were all filled with the Holy Spirit.
They preached God's message with boldness.

All the believers
were of one heart and mind."
Acts 4:24, 31-32 NLT

Amazingly, these verses don't say *some* of them in that room were united. They didn't even say *most* of them or the ones who *wanted* to be united.

It says *"**all** the believers"* in the building where they were meeting were of "one heart and mind." Paul captured how important this Word-based unity is when he reminded the Corinthians:

> "Jesus died for all that they who live should no longer live for themselves, but for Him who died and rose again on their behalf."
>
> 2 Corinthians 5:15 NASB

What's hard though is that when we resolutely decide to honor the Father and His Word, we can suffer for doing the right thing. That's why Jesus told us to "count the cost" Luke 14:28 NLT, if we want to live for Him and be used by Him.

For example...

There will be moments when we no longer can join in with what is happening all around us if we feel it will grieve the Father's heart.

People are not always going to understand why we won't let them talk to us about other people behind their back. This includes many Christians. Then no matter how sincerely kind we are when we express this, it can still be offensive.

Some may even feel we are being unloving when we won't listen to them talk about their problems with another person.

There are those who can become so miffed by our unwillingness to listen that they will speak ugly words, including untruths about us to others. We could even lose relationships we wanted to keep by making these hard choices.

But the Father encourages us that whatever it costs us, it's worth it because He promises:

"If you cling to your life, you will lose it.
But if you give it up for Me, you will find it."
Matthew 10:39 NLT

As a young Christian, I was oblivious to how God felt about all this. For example, I thoroughly enjoyed reading this account in the life of the Prophet Isaiah:

"In the year King Uzziah died I saw the Lord. He was sitting on a lofty throne and the train of His robe filled the temple. Hovering over Him were mighty Seraphim, each with six wings. In a great chorus they sang, 'Holy, holy, holy is the Lord Almighty! The whole earth is filled with His glory!'

The glorious singing shook the Temple to its foundations and the entire sanctuary was filled with smoke. I said, 'My destruction is sealed, for I am a sinful man and a member of a sinful race. I am a man of unclean lips, and I live among a people of unclean lips. Yet I have seen the King, the Lord Almighty.'

One of the Seraphim flew over to the altar and he picked up a burning coal with a pair of tongs. He touched my lips with it and said, 'See, this coal has touched your lips. Now your guilt is removed and your sins are forgiven.' Then I heard the Lord asking, 'Whom should I send as a messenger to My people? Who will go for Us?' I said, 'Lord, I'll go! Send me!' And He said, 'Yes, go.'"

Isaiah 6:1-9 NLT

What grieves me is I only saw this as a beautifully written story. There was never any application of it in my own life. It was just entertaining head knowledge. Only years later was I convicted that God had the Prophet Isaiah write that message to make a very strong point about the seriousness of the sins of the tongue. Yet for a long time, I didn't "get it." As a result, while I was enjoying how poetically Isaiah wrote about the glory of God and His Visitation, and I was involved in many times of deeply moving corporate worship and many powerful prayer meetings, I was speaking criticisms to others about my pastor. I did this even though I had been saved long enough to be aware of these verses that warn what a serious mistake this is:

"Gossip separates the best of friends. Do not associate with a gossip. For whoever secretly slanders his neighbor, him I will destroy. Remember this! In the last days there will be many troubles because people will gossip. Stay away from those people. For there are seven things I oppose and are an abomination to Me. One of them is the person who spreads strife among My people. Therefore if anyone causes divisions among My people, that person has turned away from the truth and condemned himself."

Titus 3:10-11 NLT
Proverbs 20:19, 16:28, 6:16-19 NASB
Psalm 101:5 NASB/NLT, 2 Timothy 3:1, 3, 5 NCV
Personalized

I vividly recall when I began to experience the sobering consequence of God opposing me because I had spoken against others. A long season of sadness and painful loss began in my spirit. God's blessing on His plan for my life was gone and I knew it. I was confused about what was causing all this painful, disheartening loss. I had no idea that I was paying a price for betraying the Father with my tongue and ears, and for causing division in His church. I was blind to all this because I had never taken seriously what the Word says about the destructiveness of gossip.

So my spiritual emptiness continued.

It actually took several years for me to realize that I had allowed a compartment in my mind where I had rationalized that certain scriptures didn't apply to me, such as the ones about the tongue. As a result of that choice, I brought on myself the same darkness in this serious warning:

"Anyone who is double minded is like a wave in the sea, blown up and down by the wind. They should not think they will receive anything from the Lord."

James 1:6-8 NASB/NCV

Eventually I was humbled and broken by seeing what I had done and I went to the pastor I had spoken against to tell him how deeply sorry I was. But it was too late.

The damage could not be reversed. Division had shattered the relationships in that church family. The flock was scattered with wounds that for many to this very day never healed. This special man with the Father's love for His children never pastored again. When he died, his wife said what killed him was his heart was broken.

The young people who were there helplessly watched people they looked up to and trusted hurting and betraying one another. So much was ripped away from them at a vulnerable time in their lives when they needed the Family of God to help them and encourage them.

What's so sad is that though all this took place decades ago, most of them still want nothing to do with Christianity. So generations were even affected because they are raising their own children without Jesus.

Consequently, whenever I read the story in Isaiah 6 about the prophet's brokenness, I'm affected, especially because of the damage to those youth that continues to this day. Yet I'm also comforted in securely knowing that it makes the Father very happy to forgive His children. This is one of the verses He used to help me understand that He really does feel this way so that I could heal from the regret and grief I felt when the faces of those innocent, vulnerable young people flashed across my mind:

"I didn't send My Son into your life in order to judge you, reject you, condemn you, or pass sentence on you.

I sent My son to you so that you might find Salvation, and be made safe and sound through Him."

John 3:17 Amplified

It's hugely reassuring to know that God doesn't look for people to use who haven't made serious mistakes. He made this clear through the compassion He had on Peter after he publicly betrayed Jesus and he was so devastated and sorry. I'm also deeply grateful that when we change what we talk about and just as importantly what we listen to, we can have peace and a courage that gets us through the worst times in life "because we now have hope." Job 11:18 NLT

But most of all, the Father longs to be our closest Friend and I never want to lose intimacy with Him again. I don't want worship to be something I can enter into, be moved by, and bask in enjoying. Yet while I am in His presence adoring Him, I am not broken, humbled and sorry about those things that grieve Him, like happened to Isaiah.

Deciding to do my own thing in any area of my life, including betraying love through what I talk about is not worth this terrible loss of genuine closeness. Nothing is worth me being disconnected from what pleases God and His Word, while I am having a great time singing glorious songs of worship to Him.

Therefore, I no longer ignore these verses. They actually have become a part of what matters a great deal to me:

"The tongue is a small thing, but what enormous damage it can do. A tiny spark can set a great forest on fire. The tongue is a flame of fire. It is full of wickedness that can ruin your whole life. It can turn the entire course of your life into a blazing flame of destruction. It is set on fire by hell itself. For *death* and *life* are in the power of the tongue."

James 3:5-6 NLT, Proverbs 18:21 NASB

Ever since I've been broken by my failures in this area, I've had a better understanding about why Joshua was earnest when he alerted the Israelites:

> "Get up! Command the people to purify themselves. For this is what the Lord says: **Hidden** among you are things set apart for the Lord. You will never defeat your enemies until you remove these things."
>
> Joshua 7:13 NLT

I learned the hard way that one of the "hidden" things that can take root in a believer's heart is feeling that it's alright, in certain circumstances, to not apply the Word to our own life. For example, the Bible encourages us to seek out wise, godly counsel. But this means going to someone who has the appropriate authority for us to speak to them about people so that it is not gossip, such as a pastor, church leader, ministry leader or trained counselor. If we are married, we can talk to our spouse about our struggles with people because a husband and wife are "one flesh."

Nonetheless, many still feel...

> "The verses about gossip couldn't possibly apply to me when I'm talking to my friend. I should be able to talk to someone I am close to about anyone I'm having a hard time with. There's nothing wrong with me doing this because it gives me a place to get help for the problems I'm having with people, including my pastor and people in my church."

Yet any conversation that does not honor the Word is one that grieves the Father.

This is how my husband, Barry vulnerably describes what changed him in this area of his character:

"I first started going to church at the age of twelve. For years I spent a lot of time studying the Bible. But I didn't understand anything about how to love. So I used what I learned to criticize other people. This turned me into an arrogant bully. In short, I was an unkind, judgmental jerk. The problems this lack of love caused surfaced for me in the 1980's when I was a teacher at a Christian High School where I used my head knowledge to be mean and critical.

Eventually I turned on my pastor by pointing out his flaws to whoever would listen. The teachers' lounge was a nest of people with the same critical spirit. So I had many companions in my efforts to tear him down.

After several years of sowing discord in this church, I began to see that my Christianity was phony. I struggled for two years with this realization and then the Holy Spirit convicted me that I wasn't even a believer.

When the conviction got unbearable, I told my family that I was going away to have it out with God and that I would not be back unless I got the answer I was looking for. That was a Friday afternoon. I explained all this to one of the pastors at the church and he let me use his office for my battle with God. I spent about thirty six hours complaining and arguing with God.

Finally, I told Him to either give me all He had or leave me alone and I meant it! Well, He did give me all I could handle at the time and I became a true child of God.

And yes, this changed me.

I went home and explained to my family what happened and that I regretted all the damage that my wrong way of looking at life and people had caused.

I also called the pastor and met with him. He assured me that he accepted my apology. Yet I told him I needed to make a public apology. The next morning I apologized in the two church services to about 1,500 people.

From that day on I worked very hard to control my tongue. With God's help and a lot of hard work to make very different choices, I changed in this area.

But the damage from my lack of knowing how to show love continued to affect me for several more years. My unkind, uncaring words had hurt my wife and damaged our marriage and I still didn't know how to genuinely love her. I had no idea how to show her that I cared about her feelings.

My being harsh, at times, with my children also had caused resentment, anger and deep hurts in their relationship with me.

Then although I made many sincere attempts to be different, and though getting saved had drastically changed me, I was still only into knowledge and not relationship.

The final result of me being a jerk was that I lost everything that was important to me.

The hurts that I caused my family with my unkind tongue during my years of being unloving eventually destroyed my marriage. I lost knowing my three kids. This devastated me.

When my marriage fell apart, I was pretty much alone.

I spent a lot of time with God trying to figure out what happened. He slowly began to help me see and once I got a grip on what was missing, He began to teach me.

For one year I had a crash course in what love is.

During that time, I went from zero, to having a basic understanding and after having no clue for thirty-four years of my life, I made a commitment to keep learning how to love.

I do wish I could say that the rest of the story had a happy ending.

It didn't.

None of this fixed my family.

The hurts caused by my choices could not be repaired.

The collapse of my marriage, the loss of my children and finally learning how to love took place during the two years before I knew Ruth. So by the time we met, I was a different man. My words were kind and this helped her to feel close to me as her best friend.

I also never again wanted to bring harm to the Bride of Christ and damage unity or love by speaking against her shepherds and leaders."

Barry Johnson

In the light of these insights into what can destroy unity and love in the church and in relationships, God is speaking this Message to His people:

"I'm appearing to you this day as I did to Joshua.

This is a sacred and holy moment in your life.

For I am pleading with you, as a Holy God, to ask Me to show you what's hidden in your heart and in your thinking that's betraying Me and My Word.

I'm also urging you to humble yourself before Me about what I show you. As you bow your life and heart in My presence on this hallowed ground, I've come to encounter you this very moment.

But not only as the Commander of the Lord's Army.

I'm also here as your kind, forgiving Dad.

That's why nothing would make Me happier than to give you a new start, a fresh beginning, and restore you to all the closeness that I long to have with you.

It's urgent that this happen for you because as your Father, I care deeply about you. I don't want you to continue wandering, feeling lost and discouraged.

I only want you to live to the fullest this promise I'm declaring over you, every moment of your life that 'I know the plans I have for you, plans to prosper you and not to harm you, plans to give you hope and a future.'"

- Your Father and your very real Dad

Jeremiah 29:11 NIV

Chapter Three

GOD'S GLORY ARISING

There is the deepest kind of discouragement in more and more of God's own children. The path they've been on is littered with unfulfilled dreams, broken relationships and disappointments. They know and love Jesus. But they are adrift in life, with no sense of purpose, though they long for their life to have meaning.

Many started out enthusiastically pursuing what they felt God wanted them to be. But somewhere along the way the last flicker of hope about what they thought their life was going to look like has gone out.

What's heartbreaking for my husband, Barry and me is how much it's the younger generation who are feeling this way. Though only in their twenties and early thirties, they already think that somehow they've "missed it" when it comes to God using them. Yet they've only begun their Journey of experiencing the Father's destiny for them.

Many in the older generation are also suffering tremendously with this same disheartening struggle. Only they are at the end of life when they don't have a lot of years ahead of them for the "big thing" they want to do for God to still happen. Often they had received prophecies when they were younger about those really "big" plans happening.

But when the years go by and those prophetic words are not fulfilled at all, then thinking about them only hurts. So it grieves Barry and I whenever we see this same misconception of what it looks like for God to use us hurting another generation of young people. In fact, during the months when this book was being written, we were part of the Prayer Team at a large conference for youth. This is how Barry describes what saddened us:

"We had the privilege of speaking with many of the youth. It was a joy to be able to love on these young people who are the future of the Body of Christ. Yet, it broke my heart to hear the pain, disillusionment and despair in their hearts.

After the first night, I wept as I lay on my bed. My heart ached as I recalled the look I saw in the eyes of a twenty-eight year old woman as she explained that she felt like she had failed the Lord. She explained that as a child and teen she had a fire in her heart to be a missionary. She even had opportunities to go on missions trips. But, now she felt like a failure because nothing like what she had dreamed about was happening. She also felt that because of her mistakes she had already ruined any hope of God being able to use her. She felt like her chance to be what He wanted her to be was already over.

The Lord gave me these simple words for her: 'You are still very young.' She began to weep. Then she broke down in sobs. The Lord had me repeat those same words several times. After a while I could see some hope return to her eyes as she realized the truth that it was not too late for God to use her.

As Ruth and I encouraged her, she also began to understand that no matter what our age or other circumstances, God has a 'hope and a future' for us.

For the rest of the conference, Ruth and I ministered to many young people. Most of them had the same torment in their souls.

The Lord showed me that these youth were being battered on every side by the unhealthy things that are happening in the Body of Christ as a result of our 'modern' society. The pressure caused by the over emphasis on achieving the 'big thing' has brought on feelings of failure and insignificance. This is causing so many to feel lost and useless. And they have no understanding about how to overcome the guilt from their regrets.

Their need is so great to be encouraged.

And they need to know how merciful and forgiving the Father is about our failures. They seriously need to know Him as their kind, caring Dad.

My heart broke that weekend as I realized how deep these feelings are in the younger generation.

That's when the Lord spoke to me about the need for Ruth and I to refocus our ministry on reaching these broken young people and challenging those in our generation to become fathers and mothers in the faith to them."

Barry Johnson

When I was thirty, a new Christian and on fire for God, I was one of those confused young people whom Barry and I encountered at that conference. Many began giving me encouraging personal prophecies. I especially hung on to the ones that told me I was going to do something "big and important" for God. They gave my life meaning during my hard times. But they also began to appeal to my pride and ego.

That's when the places in the Bible I enjoyed thinking about the most were the ones that supported my pursuit of fulfilling those prophecies. As time went on, these were some of the scriptures that I skipped over when I read the Bible because I **didn't** find them "inspiring" or "fun" to focus on:

"All who make themselves great will be made humble.

But all who make themselves humble will be great. Whoever wants to be a leader among you must be your servant. Therefore you must decrease and I, the Lord your God must increase. It is not the person who commends himself who is approved, but he whom I commend.

For there will be no pride allowed on My Holy Mountain, the place where My presence is. The proud will not be allowed to stand in My presence. I keep My distance from the proud. And where ever there is jealousy and selfish ambition, there you will find disorder and every kind of evil."

Luke 22:27, Matthew 20:26, John 3:30, Psalm 138:6, 5:5,
Zephaniah 3:11 NLT, 2 Corinthians 10:18 NASB
James 3:15-16 NLT
Personalized

The Holy Spirit tried many times to use each of those verses to warn me that I was going the wrong direction. But I was not open to listening. I just kept skipping over them so that I could enjoy the ones that reinforced how much God was going to use me in really "big" and "important" ways.

I also thought a lot about the prophetic words people gave me that told me how anointed I was, how powerful my calling was and what great and mighty things I was going to do for God some day. I was blind to the fact that when prophetic words end up appealing to our ego, then pride and spiritual ambition can become what guide our perspective on life and ministry. Then without even realizing it, we can try to make those things happen while we drift further and further away from what matters the most to the Father.

When I look back on the years I lost my way in all this mixed up thinking, I actually thought I was sincerely pursuing what pleased God. But I was so deceived I had no clue what He really wanted. As a result, I walked on by the people He tried to nudge me to "see" and love for Him, including when I was at church, and even after some of the most amazing worship services that were incredibly inspiring and thoroughly enjoyable. It's as if what matters the most to the Father that He makes so clear in His Word didn't even exist. I had my focus so much on doing something really "important" for God that loving a few people at a time definitely didn't fit that picture.

For example, a small women's group invited me to speak. They had heard about my ministry on the harp and how it brings the presence of God and they were excited about me coming. But when I found out there would be few attending, I turned down the invitation. I still remember their faces. They were humble women in a small church.

The Father was asking me to bring my prophetic gifting to encourage them. But I had completely lost sight of what is most important to Him and it wasn't me using my gifting or my anointing in impressive ways.

What makes Him happy is when we are like the Samaritan who cared about the man on the side of the road, rather than walking on by him on a quest for God to use me in "big" ways.

As time went by with me doing a lot of "important" speaking engagements for large crowds in the Western United States, I felt increasingly more empty and confused.

I was often battered by this troubling thought:

"A train that represented God's destiny for me had somehow come to town and I had missed the train. And it wasn't coming back into my town again."

But all this changed one morning in March of 2000.

I became so troubled that I cried out to God through many tears: "Your Word says that only those with clean hands and pure hearts can climb Your Holy Mountain and be close to You in Your Holy Place. Oh God, please do for me what You did for David. Search my heart and show me what's wrong. Expose what's in my heart that's grieving You."

The moment that prayer ended, He answered me and my heart was broken as He showed me the person I had become.

All I could do was weep and tell the Father:

"I'm so sorry. This isn't where I wanted to end up at all when Jesus first found me. I was so full of love for You. Please forgive me. Please give me another chance."

But even as I poured all this out to the Father, I wondered how He could ever forgive all my failures and wrong choices that had taken me far away from what He meant for me to be. It was hard for me to believe that He really would give me another chance. But His gentle compassion interrupted my crushing uncertainty.

These are the words He spoke to me and what He showed me is how He feels toward anyone who longs to be free of regret and guilt.

"My child, *any* moment you ever come to Me broken, humbled and sorry, I forgive you. I cleanse you from every wrong. I do this so thoroughly, I don't remember any of it. Even if you come another time to tell Me how sorry you are for that same mistake, I will only say to you, 'What are you talking about? For Me, as your Dad, none of this exists anymore.'

You are that completely forgiven. You knowing this and becoming secure that this is truly how much I love you will greatly help you to forgive yourself. This means that whenever you tell Me you are truly sorry, you are set free. Your life is pure white, like freshly fallen snow. Everything you are sorry for is removed from you, as far as the east is from the west. It's all swept away just as completely as the morning mist disappears when the sun comes up.

My Son fully paid the price to set you this completely free. And as your Father who loves you with kindness and understanding, it always makes Me happy to give you this new beginning.

So be at peace. Everything's going to be alright. I'm gently holding your right hand and saying to you, 'Don't be afraid. I will help you.'

I also want to encourage you that I used Peter and David in the fullness of My purpose for them *after* they failed.

I never held against them their failures. They only experienced the mistakes they most deeply regretted being washed away as if they never happened. This is what I will always do for you too.

So be encouraged. The winter of your soul is past. The rains have come and gone. It's the springtime of your life and a new beginning.

Therefore, My child arise and come with Me into the destiny I have for you. Flowers of beautiful new life are bursting from their buds all around you.

Your season for singing and renewed hope has come."

Your Father and your Dad

Isaiah 1:18, 44:22, 41:13 NLT
1 John 1:9, John 6:20 NLT/NASB
Song of Solomon 2:10-12 NASB
Psalms 103:12, 65:8 NCV
Jeremiah 31:34 NLT

For the longest time, I cried while it sunk in that this is the kind of Father whom God truly is. I felt such awe as I told Him:

"Lord, You really do understand how much we need Your reassurance when all we can see is our failures. You do know how insecure we can feel when we regret what we've become. Yet we feel helpless about how to find our way to Your freedom and peace."

Experiencing that much unconditional kindness caused the most comforting peace I've ever known to settle on my soul. Yet as I stepped into this new beginning with God, I also knew He was showing me these insights into His heart that He didn't want me to **ever** forget:

"It's **not** how gifted or anointed any of My children are that matters the most to Me.

It's not even My plan for them, though I long to help each one to fully live My purpose for them.

What I cherish, most of all, is when one of My sons or daughters wants to be close to Me in My presence. Not to perform. Not to do anything at all sometimes. Not to always get something from Me, though I care greatly about all his needs. But to be with Me as My friend.

What also means **just as much** is when a child of Mine wants to love others with the **same** longing and passion as when they sing their most glorious worship to Me or they pray fervently about what matters the most to Me."

Life, closeness to God, enjoying incredible corporate worship and being in passionate prayer meetings have never looked the same since I realized all this.

Another place of breakthrough that deeply affected me was that I had only emphasized me trusting God. I had no idea how much it mattered to Him if He could trust me.

Seeing this stirred up a Radical Awakening in my soul that shook me at my foundation.

Then it was this glimpse into the tragic defeat of Saul's destiny that the Father used to show me how heartbreaking it is for Him when He no longer can trust us.

Saul was the most anointed and gifted man of his time. Even the Prophet Samuel said of him: "There is no one like him among the people." Yet over and over Saul did whatever he wanted and not what God told him to do.

When he was confronted by Samuel about his disobedience, Saul only had excuses. He was quick to rationalize why it was alright for him to not honor what God said was very important to Him. He learned nothing from being told by the Prophet how wrong he was. Finally God said with a broken heart, "I am sorry I made Saul king because he has stopped following Me."

Samuel was so upset by hearing how God felt that he wept all night long.

To make all this even more troubling, when he went to look for Saul the next morning, he was told by the people that he had "gone to Carmel, to build a monument to his honor."

When Samuel found him, all Saul did was once again explain away his betrayal of what God had told him to do. He even claimed he had obeyed the Lord. Sadly, this powerfully anointed, exceptionally gifted man couldn't be wrong.

There was no brokenness.

No repentance.

Only the defensiveness of pride and arrogance.

Eventually Samuel said to him: "The Lord has torn the kingdom of Israel from you today. He has given it to one of your neighbors who is better than you. For disobedience is as bad as the sin of witchcraft. Pride is as bad as the sin of worshipping a false god."

1 Samuel 10:24-25, 13:7-14, 15:1-35 NLT/NCV
Excerpts / Paraphrased

What really caught my attention was that although God no longer trusted Saul, he could still prophesy with such authority that the people continued to call him a Prophet. This puzzled me until I remembered that the "gifts and calling of God are irrevocable." Romans 11:29 NASB Therefore, He doesn't take back our calling and gifting, no matter how seriously without character we use them. But what's lost is exactly what happened to Saul.

God's presence and His blessing on Saul's destiny were no longer on him. The Father no longer trusted him. All this gifted man had left was the emptiness of being powerfully anointed.

I was overcome with grief as I saw all this.

In many ways I had gone the same direction in my own ambition, pride and self-importance. Like Saul, I often saw miracles when people were affected by my gifting and anointing.

But I had no clue how grieved the Father was that His blessing and His presence couldn't be on anything I did for Him because He *no longer trusted me.*

That sad loss happened because what meant the most to me was not the humble character that His Son made very clear in these words is what matters the most to His Father:

"I only do what I see You, as My Father doing. For My Father, You love Me. You tell Me everything You are doing. I don't even speak on My own authority because You, My Father are the one who sent Me. You are the one who gave Me Your own instructions as to what I should say and do. And I know Your instructions lead to eternal life. Because I lived like this, I brought glory to You here on earth and having done all that You brought Me into Your glory. For I am gentle and humble in heart."

John 5:19, 17:4-5, Matthew 11:29

During the years when I was blind to all my deception, I had read many times that God's "ways are not our ways and His thoughts are not anything like our thoughts." Isaiah 55:8-9 Yet now I finally saw that what I had valued as "big and important" was far, far away from any of God's ways of looking at His sons and daughters serving Him.

For even though Jesus did speak to thousands at times, He spent most of His time loving one leper, one guilt-ridden woman, one distressed young man and one child at a time. Therefore there's nothing "bigger" than loving people each moment that is possible.

Another practical insight that I finally began to grasp is that few are called or anointed to have a big ministry that reaches thousands. Therefore, for a lot of people to hope for that is setting themselves up to be crushed by discouragement and even devastated by false expectations.

Then the more disillusioned they become when what they expected does not happen, they are increasingly more vulnerable to ending up in the darkness of despair. It also was pretty shocking when I first saw that at the end of His life, Jesus only had eleven men and a few faithful women who were solidly with Him. In the Upper Room, there were only 120 of His followers.

So Jesus' ministry was not "big" at all based on what many in our current Christian culture view as doing something "important."

Then by approximately 55 A.D. many of the early believers had lost sight of loving like Jesus gave His very life to teach us.

This is when the Apostle Paul tried so hard, as a father in the faith, to help them return to their Christian roots when he wrote to the Corinthians these honest, blunt words:

> "If I could speak in any language in heaven or on earth, but didn't love others, I would only be making meaningless noise like a loud gong or a clanging cymbal. If I had the Gift of Prophecy, and if I knew all the mysteries of the future and knew everything about everything, but didn't love others, what good would I be? And if I had the gift of faith so that I could speak to a mountain and make it move, without love I would be no good to anybody. If I didn't love others, I would be of no value whatsoever."
>
> 1 Corinthians 13:1-3 NLT

Sadly, in Christianity today we are up against the same issues that unraveled the Book of Acts Revival and caused what Jesus taught to become a distant memory.

This is why the Father longs for this to be the generation that returns to what He and His Son feel the most passionately about.

When Barry and I lived and ministered extensively in Africa, we actually witnessed what can happen when there is a restoration to the love of the Gospels.

This is one of those amazing stories...

On Mt Elgon in East Africa, there was a man who was considered by many as the most powerful spiritual leaders on the Mountain. The other pastors were terrified to be in the same room with him because he had falsely accused them and they ended up in jail. That's a brutal place to be among this remote tribe where violence was a deadly part of their lives.

Barry met with this key leader. He spoke into his life about the destructive competition and jealousies that were dividing the leaders and causing the unbelievers to want nothing to do with Christianity. There was a powerful reconciliation between this man and the other pastors. Then during one of our large meetings, these men publicly humbled themselves, forgave one another and wept in each other's arms. What we saw that night reminded me of what God expressed in these powerful words:

"If My people who are called by My name will humble themselves and pray. If they will seek My face and turn from their wicked ways. I will hear from heaven and forgive their sins. I will restore their land."
2 Chronicles 7:14

Yet even if we do all this, **only** if there's a return of Christians to loving one another can any move of God **continue.**

That is actually a major reason that Azusa Street could last for three years and spread to the nations. Frank Bartleman, an eye witness historian of that Revival describes how strong the conviction of the Holy Spirit was on the people about protecting love:

"A high standard was held up on Azusa. God's love was wonderfully manifest in the meetings. The leaders would not even allow an unkind word said against those who opposed them. The message was the love of God. It was like the first love of the early church had returned. We knew the moment we had grieved the Spirit by an unkind thought or word. The presence of the Lord was so real." *Frank Bartleman*

A lack of this kind of love among the Christians on Mt Elgon was the greatest obstacle to the miraculous move of God on the Mountain continuing.

This is how the Father used tragic suffering to help the people see the seriousness of that hindrance. A boy suddenly appeared during a morning session. His mother was a vilely hated Karamajong warrior. When she died, everyone turned on her son, including his father and the Christians on Mt. Elgon. Wherever this child went, he was beaten. After years of such violent treatment, he was deformed. He couldn't speak or walk.

All he could do was crouch low and shuffle from place to place, as he moaned like a wounded animal.

Yet underneath his marred, mangled body and misshapen face was a heart that hurt with the same horrific pain that anyone feels who is cruelly mistreated and they have no one to love them.

This strange looking boy now suddenly appeared from nowhere the night when God's glory descended upon the Mountain. He painfully crawled toward the harp and sat down close to me. When I glanced down, there was a horrifying sadness in his eyes. He moaned in the most heartbreaking way, as if he were begging me: "Please don't send me away."

Several agitated leaders in the church walked toward the boy. Overcome by the agony in the Father's heart over this boy's horrendous suffering, I firmly motioned to them to let him stay.

Moments later while I was teaching, he suddenly appeared again. He sat down in the aisle very close to my feet while he imploringly looked up at me with those same desperately pleading eyes. This time I was able to kneel down in front of him on the dirt floor, hold his hands and smile to reassure him, while I told the people in almost a whisper: "The love Jesus talks about isn't just for those we want to be close to. It also means reaching out to the outcast, the leper, and those no one wants to love."

I paused as I sensed a resentful resistance in the room.

"We must love that way," I continued, "or what God did last night will not last and that would be a tragic loss for the Mountain." But the believers continued to push the boy away.

Whenever they stood up to greet one another, he reached out with his deformed arms. He ached for someone to please love him, too.

But everyone ignored his desperate pleas. Each time this tormented boy tried to come into the room, the men dragged him outside, threw him into the dirt and beat him. He longingly stared from a distance while they ate. No one would give him anything to eat, despite his mournful wails of unspeakable pain.

That night our team sat together and reflected on what had taken place. Our hearts were heavy about the young boy as one of the young men poured out his heart:

> "The moment that affected me the most this week was when Mama Ruth drew that boy close to her at the end of tonight's session.
> The people stared at her with shock.
>
> They couldn't believe what they were seeing because for years he had rummaged like a wild animal through rotting garbage for all his food. The only bath he'd had since his mother died was the rain falling on him. He was covered with the worst kinds of filth, including dried urine and human feces. The smell was ghastly.
>
> All of us could see maggots crawling all over him as Mama Ruth held him close to her.
>
> The believers were horrified to watch this.

They also knew he had terrible diseases that caused people to even more cruelly shun him. No one was willing to touch him, except to beat him. Yet she wrapped this boy in her arms and drew him close to her.

This is a picture of God's love that the people of this Mountain will never be able to forget. I know for the rest of my life, I will never forget it."

With an ache in our hearts, the weeks of ministry ended on the Mountain. Barry and I hoped that what God did was so powerful, it would change how the Christians treated one another. We especially wanted this to happen for the boy.

So we were greatly encouraged when a group of women who were highly respected in their tribe decided to adopt him like he was their son.

They united to be kind to him. We actually observed this taking place when the boy came to our tent to say goodbye to us. These women did something that was unheard of. They smiled at him and offered him food. His squeals of delight and bright, happy smiles were priceless. Watching him made us all cry.

Then several weeks after our time of ministry on the Mountain, we received the encouraging news that the unsaved were dancing in the streets after they saw the leaders going to one another, weeping and repenting.

Many of the churches and across denominations were growing. The unbelievers were coming into the services asking how to be born again.

Frank Bartleman captures the kind of heart and character that were a core part of the Revival on Azusa Street and that also made it possible for this supernatural move of God to come upon a Mountain in Africa:

"The people who really humble themselves, God will release to do His work.

For He who prepares His work through the ages accomplishes it by using the weakest instruments. He does this so that the work may be seen to be of God and not of man. For a great work of God is never accomplished by the natural strength of man. That's why there is always much need of heart preparation, in humility and consecration, before God can come.

It's why the depth of any move of God will be determined exactly by the spirit of repentance that is present. In fact, that is the key to every true move of God.

A true Pentecost will always produce a mighty conviction of sin and a turning to God. That's why we must keep humble and little in our own eyes.

If we get built up by a sense of our own importance, we are gone. God has always sought a humble people. He can use no other.

But lo, our God comes.

He will not keep silent." Frank Bartleman

At this time in the history of God's people, once again He will not keep silent. Darkness is ominously increasing across the nations. Our God yearns to come again with His glory.

Even now, He is declaring this Message.
His voice is that of a loud Trumpet

"Look at the nations and be amazed. Watch and be astounded. I am going to do something in your own day, something you wouldn't believe even if someone told you about it.

Therefore My people, I urge you to come close to Me. Come with a longing to seek My face. And hear the sound of heaven. Join all heaven in worshipping Me as they sing the New Song of the Lamb before My throne. For as My people draw close to Me, I am going to pour out, as never before, My mighty miracles, My supernatural deliverances, My healings to set people free from the desperation of their pain.

The good news about My Son Jesus is going to spread. A revelation of Me as a kind, caring Father is going to transform the lives of the fatherless across the generations and the nations.

But even as I'm earnestly searching for those with a longing to worship Me and to fervently cry out to Me in prayer, I ache for them to have the **same** passion to love others for Me. These are **equally** important to Me. They **each** need to happen for the fullness of My coming upon the nations to be possible.

Because if you worship Me with all your heart and soul and might, and if you earnestly pray about what matters the most to Me, My heart is broken if you are not just as dedicated to loving others for Me, and the fullness of what I long to do among My people is tragically hindered.

I am also searching for simple, ordinary women and men, young and old, to bring this same healing, redeeming love to the desperately lost, the hurting, the despairing, and those who need My hope for their troubled souls.

But to prepare the way for this new Wind of My Spirit and this coming of My glory, I need My people to humble themselves. I need those who are My children to come to Me with brokenness about anything in your hearts that could hinder My Revival from coming again upon My church.

I need you to be deeply convicted of all ambition, pride, sins against love, and any damage to the unity in My church you are responsible for so that when I do come, My Holy Fire can spread far and wide. Only those who are broken in repentance for anything they are doing that is grieving Me can I use with My favor upon the plan and destiny I have for them in this crucial hour in all of Christianity.

And I am coming.

Yet it is with the Consuming Fire of My Glory.

In that Holy Fire, only the humble will be raised up to do My mighty works.

Only those who know to the depths of their souls that they must decrease, and I must increase, can I trust to be fully used for My glorious purposes.

For I am rising upon My Church.

It's going to be a Radical Awakening.

Because of My tender mercy, a light from heaven is about to break upon My people once again. To give light to those who sit in darkness and in the shadow of death and to guide them to the path of My peace.

So arise, shine. Your light has come. My glory is arising. I'm going to appear upon you and generations will be changed by the light of My hope that you will bring to them."

- Your Father and your Dad

Luke 1:78-79, 24:7
Isaiah 54:10, 60:1 NLT/NASB
Acts 17:27 NLT/NASB
Habakkuk 1:5
Exodus 24:17

Chapter Four

LIBERATING TRUTHS

Revival *is* on the horizon.

It is stirring and it's going to burst forth.

But Revival is not a meeting.
It's not a conference.
It's not an event.
It's not a powerfully anointed speaker.

Revival is a Radical Awakening in a child of God which transforms our character so that we can carry the presence of God and His love everywhere we go.

Then as the signs and wonders and miracles of Jesus follow us, there is a lasting impact.

What you are about to read are some of the crucial changes we need to make so that we can be carriers of the presence of God in this powerful way.

These areas of personal growth are vital because God needs each of us during this critical time in Christianity to be part of spreading the fire of His Revival to others.

This is my honest account about how I had to change and grow. I share it in the hope that it can help others who need these insights to find their way to those same places of transformation.

Excerpts from Ruth's book:
"The Trip to Freedom"

By the time I was thirty years old, I experienced every type of brutally scarring abuse.

As a result, I hated men. I feared and mistrusted women. I never felt completely safe with anyone.

Frightening nightmares terrified me whenever I tried to sleep. An irrational panic consumed my thoughts. Fear imprisoned me. Haunting memories bombarded me. Remembering the painful, graphic details of the terrible things that had happened to me and my brother and sister constantly replayed in my mind. Rage simmered inside me. At times it came out in uncontrollable explosions of destructive anger. Thoughts of killing myself consumed me.

No one knew about the terrifying abuse I was living with or how I felt about anything. Emotional honesty didn't feel safe at all. All of this caused me to shrink back from reality. I isolated myself. There was the smiling person people saw in public, and the disturbed one who lived inside of me. The stress of all this began to affect me physically. A doctor told me I had the beginnings of many serious health issues and I had better do something about what was going on in my life that could cause all this damage. But as I listened to him warn me, I saw no way I could get free from the torment I was hiding from everyone.

After being betrayed and violated, over and over, as a child by those who were supposed to be safe for me to trust, fragile places on the inside of me had died a long time ago.

The damage felt irreversible.

In the midst of this personal nightmare, I never thought it would be possible to put it all behind me and not have it control my life anymore. Yet that transformation did happen.

What took place is a message of hope for all who ache to be set free from devastating pain and fully enter into the fullness of the Father's destiny for them.

I Forgive

No child wants to hate his parents. When we do, something dies in our soul that we seriously need to be a whole person. That death remains until we forgive. If we refuse to, this choice is deadly. It can cause us physical illness and even thrust us into the alarming, dark shadows of being emotionally disturbed.

This is how that happened for me.

A long time before I became a Christian, I made up my mind I'd never forgive my parents for the horrible things they did to me.

Consequently, when I was saved at twenty-nine, the agony of my pain didn't stop. It actually got worse because I refused to stop being bitter. The poison of this destructive choice affected every part of my life. Through my toxic example, my daughter learned that the way you react to people who hurt you is to hate them. Eventually that hatred included me. My disastrous decision to not forgive catapulted me to the brink of a serious mental collapse.

After I had been a Christian for about two years, my world came crashing down all around me. I heard voices, but no one was actually speaking to me. Late at night I was afraid to walk past the living room. I was sure that a man was lurking in the shadows waiting to attack me. But whenever I rushed to turn on the lights, no one was there. I often woke up in a cold sweat from terrifying nightmares. In these haunting dreams, my ex-husband kept coming back to kill me.

During the day, a chilling apprehension obsessed me. Every time my children walked outside to play, I shuddered with out of control fear that they would be killed.

After one of these attacks of anxiety, I retreated to my bedroom. As I lay rigidly on my bed, I was convinced that someone was coming stealthily down the hallway toward my room. My heart raced and my body stiffened under the cold sheets. I was too terrified to make a sound. I strained to listen for footsteps. But there was only silence, except for my muffled breathing. I pulled the blanket tight under my chin and stared at the partially opened door.

"He's going to kill me!" I screamed within me as I frantically gripped the blanket. "I know there's someone out there and he's going to kill me."

I couldn't move. I could barely breathe. My disturbed mind was convinced that an intruder was there.

The alarming history of insanity on both sides of my family now raced through my mind.

"I'm going crazy," I thought, "just like so many people in my family. I'm going to end up like one of them. I'm losing my mind!"

My life was spinning out of control.

The evil forces that were trying to destroy me kept battering me with terrifying thoughts. I felt like I was suffocating in a dark tunnel of frightening panic. I tried to stop the downward spiral. But I couldn't push back the darkness that was now overtaking me. I was painfully aware that at any moment I could cross over into a place of so much mental confusion that I wouldn't be able to come back to reality.

"Oh God," I cried out. "Help me! Please help me!"

The Father's response was immediate. But it **wasn't** comforting like I had expected.

"Ruth," He told me, "you must forgive everyone who has ever hurt you, especially your mother. The hatred toward your mother is the bitter root that is destroying you."

I resisted.

"After everything my mother has done to me," I vehemently said, "I have every right to hate her. I'll forgive everyone else, but I will never forgive my mother!"

But God warned me:

"If you don't forgive her, your hatred will destroy you. And I won't be able to help you."

I jumped up from my bed, stood in the middle of the room, and shook with loud sobs. My mind was already dangerously close to slipping away from me. I couldn't go on living the way I was feeling for another second. I was determined to hang on to life as I lifted my arms like a young, trusting child.

"Oh God," I cried out. "I don't feel any forgiveness toward Mom. But I will do what You are telling me to do. I choose to forgive her. In the name of Jesus I forgive her." At first I said these words completely by faith.

I felt nothing at all.

But as I made the decision to speak them over and over, my feelings toward my mother changed. Suddenly vivid scenes from my childhood flashed through my mind. I recalled her bending over the kitchen sink, moaning in pain; being stiff and white as a corpse on her bed in her darkened room, her countenance clouded with despair; lying collapsed on the kitchen floor, unable to speak; screaming at me every time I tried to talk to her, "Shut up! Leave me alone," pushing me away whenever I tried to be close to her.

I covered my face with trembling hands and wept as I faced with full honesty how much all this had hurt me.

I then told God all about it, holding nothing back as a lifetime of pain exploded out of my soul. Suddenly, something amazing happened. My heart began to ache for my mother. Instead of seeing her as the person who had caused me so much suffering, I was able to look at her through the eyes of the Father. Compassion for her hopelessness pierced my heart. She knew I was suffering all those years when I was growing up. But she was in too much pain herself to have anything left to give to anyone. It took all she had to just survive.

Moments later, a healing I never thought was possible began to touch the most broken places in my soul. "I not only forgive her, Lord," I then told Him, "but for the first time I can finally say I love her. I forgive everyone who has ever hurt me, even though I have no feelings about doing that. I'm just deciding because I don't want to hang on to any of it anymore."

I learned I could do all this by **choice** when I read these surprising words:

> "**You** must change your heart and life. I am kind to you so that you can do this. So **choose** this day a blessing or a curse. I urge you to choose life in order that you may live."
> Acts 3:19 NCV, Romans 2:4 NCV
> Deuteronomy 30:19 NASB

I'll never forget how it struck me that God didn't say, "**Feel** this day a blessing or a curse." He said choose.

He also didn't say that **He** was in charge of doing all the changing in me. He put a lot of that responsibility on me.

Then as I decide to obey His Word in my choices, He can come in with a flood of help, just as He promises in these incredibly reassuring words: "There is no one like the God of Israel. He rides across the heavens to help you, across the skies in majestic splendor." Deuteronomy 33:26 NLT

What's sad is many people think that if they don't feel it, then it's not real forgiveness. As a result, they are trapped in their bitterness, with no way to end it. So I'll always be grateful that the Word makes it clear we only have to **decide** to forgive.

This decision can set us free from hatred, even if we feel nothing at all.

But for me all of this was the easy part. After I forgave my mother and everyone who had ever hurt me, I was only able to move on with my life when every day, many times a day, I made the determined decision to not let my mind go back to thinking about the past. I learned I had to do this from Paul when he declared:

"Brethren, I do not regard myself as having laid hold of it yet; but one thing I do. **Forgetting** what lies behind, and reaching forward to what lies ahead, I press on toward the goal for the prize of the upward call of God in Christ Jesus."

Philippians 3:13-14 NLT/NASB

Paul even explained what we have to do so that we are able to "forget," since even after we forgive those destructive thoughts can still come at our mind and trouble us all over again if we allow it.

Through these practical instructions I began to understand that Word-based "forgetting" means refusing to **think** about the hurts anymore:

> "Fix your thoughts on what is true and honorable and right. Think about things that are pure and lovely and a **good** report. Think about things that are excellent and worthy of praise. Practice these things and the God of peace will be with you. And cast down imaginations and every high thing that exalts itself against the knowledge of God. Bring into captivity **every thought** to the obedience of Christ."
>
> 2 Corinthians 10:5 KJV
> Philippians 4:8-9 NLT/NASB

As a result of learning all this from Paul, every time the oppressive remembering of past hurts tried to bombard my mind, I did all I could, just as fast as possible, to stop those thoughts "in their tracks." At the same time, I changed what I was thinking about to a "good report" such as:

What I was grateful for

A scripture that helped me to have peace

Simple, from the heart, childlike words to God about how much I love Him.

The Father helped me see that I also had to **stop talking** about the hurts because "the words I speak can cause death to come on my life and emotions." Proverbs 18:21 NCV

If that happens, the horrible pain can torment us all over again. Then we have to battle the haunting memories and what a waste of emotional energy that is. I know because there were times at the beginning of this new way of living when I did allow myself to talk about the old "stuff." But I learned very quickly that this was a big mistake and it was awful to have to fight against all the old stuff until I got back to a place of peace again.

At first, hanging on to my breakthrough was exhausting. I had to stop my thoughts and change them to a "good report" an unbelievable number of times all day long because my mind had such a life-long habit of endlessly rehearsing the hurts. To help me, I wrote down a few verses and kept them with me wherever I went. Then whenever I was taken off guard by one of these really difficult moments in my mind, I was immediately able to read them. I also memorized a few that helped me the most whenever I thought about them.

At night when I had troubling dreams, I could wake up and easily change what I was focusing on to those comforting verses.

Yet, I also discovered that no matter how diligent I was in dealing with the damage from my past, I still could get hit unexpectedly with disturbing reminders. At first whenever that happened, it felt like everything was just as bad as it used to be. Sometimes this caused me to question if I had truly forgiven or even if I had actually been healed. However, as fast as possible I told myself that all of this was a horrible lie and a vicious, demonic attack to rob me of my peace. I also very firmly reminded myself that if I allowed these lies to stay in my thoughts, I would be dragged back into a place of torment and darkness and I would be doing that to myself.

So just as quickly as if someone had thrown a hot potato at me to catch, I learned to stop negative thoughts by refusing to let my mind think them.

What's really encouraging is that as time passed, these struggles became less intense.

They occurred less often.

Gradually, being whole and healthy became my new "normal."

The poisonous venom of my hatred was gone. In all the caverns of my soul where resentment once reigned, a light now shined.

This took care of the past.

Yet then I had to learn how to deal with new, significantly painful moments that occur in the present.

For example, Mom never changed the way she treated me. Her rejection actually became increasingly more cruel. I would drive five hundred miles to visit her. After I had been with her only a few minutes she would coldly say, "You can leave now. Goodbye." Each time her pushing me away brought back an avalanche of all the pain from a lifetime of her doing this to me.

But I remembered to react to the hurt as if it was a "hot potato," by forgiving so fast that bitterness didn't have the power to get back into my heart and rob me of my peace.

Likewise, during those new times of devastating sadness and a raw sense of loss in my relationship with my mother, I also firmly reminded myself:

> "No matter how much I want Mom to love me, I can't make that happen. I will only be destroyed if I open the door again and allow myself to need her love. So I choose again to run to the kind love of God." Each time I made this decision, the Lord always reminded me: "I will comfort you just like a caring mother does for her child." Isaiah 66:13 NASB

At the same time, I had to put the new mountain of horrible grief behind me. I was able to do that by once again being completely real with myself and with God about how devastated I felt. Then just as soon as I could, that **same day** if at all possible, I passionately obeyed the Father who told me:

> "**Forget** all that.
>
> It is **nothing** compared to what I am going to do."
> Isaiah 43:18-19 NLT
> Philippians 3:12-14 NASB

These choices made it possible for me to swiftly shut the door on any new rejection from Mom and not allow it to have any power over my life. These determined decisions also kept me from feeling all over again that I had a gaping hole in my heart where a mother's love needed to be. Instead, I continued to walk in the comforting kindness of the Holy Spirit every time I got to the other side of one of these really hard experiences.

But my mother was so determined to push me out of her life that even as she faced her death, she had no room in her heart for me. She ended her days just as she had lived them, not wanting to know me or even say goodbye to me by telling my sister to never let me know she had died. To fulfill that promise, she completely disappeared from my life. I had no idea how to find her or mom. I didn't even know that my mother was gone until eight years after her death.

No words can sufficiently capture how much this hurt. Yet as I have been describing, I had learned what to do when new hurts happened and clearly understanding this is what protected my heart. So once again, I knew how to get to the other side of the overwhelming grief so that I could be at peace again. Consequently, the damage from her abandonment in no way was able to poison my soul. I was able to put the crippling sense of loss from this final, brutally cruel rejection behind me and once again embrace where the Father wanted me to go in my life. As a result, the lifetime of heartache from knowing my mother does not influence my choices in relationships. Her rejection has no power over me at all. It's as if all the tragic loss from my relationship with her never occurred. None of the pain she caused even matters to me anymore. I am loved by the best Dad in the whole world and I've found a home and a safe refuge for my heart in the kind and tender heart of God.

Yet the time to let go of all bitterness is before we make big mistakes in relationships and before we damage those we love with its toxic poison. That's why I wish I had found the liberating truth about forgiving when I was much younger. This would have changed the course of my life.

Overcoming Regret

The worst kind of pain to get over is often our regrets. That's what happened to me. Although I had forgiven everyone else in my life, I didn't know how to give that same grace and mercy to myself. Mainly because I didn't know how to stop the agony of wishing I had done things differently when I was raising my children. I kept getting battered by remembering that after they were abused in my first marriage, I put them in another unsafe home with my second husband where they were hurt in even more horrifically damaging ways.

I began to find my way out of this torment when I was able to see how God looked at my failures as a mother. This is what He showed me that is for anyone who needs this same reassuring perspective:

> "You couldn't have tried harder to be a good mom. It just was not possible. You had no more you could give. So you need to stop judging yourself by what you now realize they needed from you. You need to see that it just couldn't happen back then.
>
> You also need to encourage yourself that you **did** try your very best with what you were capable of giving to them at that time.
>
> This is how I see you. And it's how I, as your Dad, long for you to see yourself."

Once I let this kindness from the Father into my heart I finally was able to forgive myself.

But I also experienced that though the guilt was gone, it didn't mean that thinking about my regrets wouldn't hurt anymore.

For years the holidays still stirred up a world of heartache any time I was hit with what I had lost in my relationships with my children. But once I forgave myself then the pain was different. When I was full of guilt, the torment wouldn't go away. Yet now I was able to work through the emotions and get to the other side of them, and more and more quickly. I did that by reminding myself:

"I can't change the choices that I made in the past. I can only make healthy choices in the present."

Then I switched the heartbreaking thoughts to anything that gave me comfort and hope. I knew it was critical that I make this choice as soon as possible because I had spent so many years wishing I had done things differently that it was easy for me to be devastated by painful memories if I let them stay in my thoughts. So I had to be vigilantly careful not to allow myself to think about them.

Whenever they did flash through my mind uninvited and unexpectedly, I had to shut them down by *making* myself stop those thoughts and change them to whatever helped me to have the Father's comfort and peace.

During the years since this radical change in my life, I've often been strengthened by thinking about the life of Paul. He was a man who easily could have been mentally and emotionally destroyed by remembering his failures.

These are some of the horrific things he did:

Paul had the power to stop innocent Stephen from being stoned to death. But he stood there and let that man whose face shined like an angel be brutally killed.

Then after that death "a great wave of persecution began that same day. Saul went everywhere to devastate the church. He went from house to house, dragging out both men and women to throw them in jail."

After he was saved and serving the Father as an apostle, he wrote to the Corinthians how he felt about all this: "I am the least worthy of the apostles and I am not fit or deserving to be called an apostle, because I once wronged and pursued and molested the church of God, oppressing it with cruelty and violence.

You know what I was like when I followed the Jewish religion, how I violently persecuted the Christians. I did my best to get rid of them. I used to believe that I ought to do everything I could to oppose the followers of Jesus. Authorized by the leading priests, I caused many of the believers in Jerusalem to be sent to prison. And I cast my vote against them when they were condemned to death. Many times I had them whipped in the synagogues to try to get them to curse Christ.

I was so violently opposed to them that I even hounded them in distant cities of foreign lands."

1 Corinthians 15:9 AMP, Galatians 1:13
Acts 8:1-3, 26:9-11 NLT

This is a world of pain for any human being to overcome.

It's enough to haunt anyone with emotionally crippling guilt for the rest of their life.

But Paul got free!

He went on to fully live the Father's plan for him to make a difference in the lives of others. He did that by refusing to let his deeply regretted past destroy him by making up his mind to receive the Father's forgiveness. In response to that mercy, Paul found the courage to forgive himself. Then he made the hard choice to forget it all and move on with his life.

That is what I had to do also.

A Kind Dad

I lost many years going from one destructive relationship to another.

It was always my futile attempt to find the love I never received from my earthly father. I was always searching for someone to meet my needs in that shattered place inside of me. But none of these efforts ever worked. Inevitably, they ended in heartbreaking loss and made the pain worse.

Only when I let God become my very real Dad did I have a chance to learn how to make this suffering stop and amazingly that did happen. I became so whole that it was as if none of the agony of my past ever happened.

The love from my new Father restored me. His faithful kindness washed away the devastating pain from my troubled relationship with Pop. For the first time in my life, I had the courage to put behind me the grief I always felt in my relationship with him. The tormenting sadness also left. The dark cloud of overwhelming rejection from my father stopped dominating my thoughts and controlling my life. With my whole being I thirstily drank in the realization that I was an exceedingly loved child by a very real and kind Dad.

As a result, all the ways Pop broke my heart didn't matter anymore because now I have the most wonderful Dad in the whole world.

To be honest, none of this was easy to do.

It meant I had to make a lot of constant, hard choices. But my transformation did happen. The nightmare of my past was over, including the torment of my regrets.

I'm free.

I'm living my dream to serve God.

A big part of all this being possible was me getting to know Him more and more as my Father. He's the one who gave me the courage to keep on making the same healthy choices.

That's why I'm so thankful I can tell myself during the hard times that I never have to face anything again without a Dad.

But what grieves me now is that there are multitudes who are suffering because they've never experienced this love of the Father.

Yet a close relationship with Him as a kind Dad is the only way any of His kids can be fully restored in the places deep on the inside of them where bitterness and regrets can destroy them.

He is the only one who can take us by the hand and show us the path to His freedom.

What's also reassuring is that I've experienced for a long time and in many situations that the Father is always kind. He never condemns us, no matter how much we've "blown it." He lets us know whenever we are going the wrong direction and helps us find our way back. And He's never too busy to be there for us whenever we need a Father's encouragement and support.

For those who have never experienced this amazing love of the Father, it's one of the reasons they are hurting with sadness and emptiness in their soul.

It's also why life can feel scary and confusing at times for so many sincere believers.

Not having a father who loved us when we were young can cause all this. Because God gives us an earthly dad to be a steadying source of wisdom and understanding while we try to find our way in life.

We especially need this fatherly help when we begin young adulthood and there are so many new challenges that can get really confusing, even troubling to figure out by ourselves.

But if we were hurt by our dad growing up, we may not be interested at all in having that kind of relationship with God.

I certainly didn't want it when I began my life as a Christian.

He compassionately understands these feelings and wants us to be fully real with Him about them. So if this is what you want to do, I encourage you to ask Him to become your Dad. You may not have any feelings about it and that's totally alright. But what you are doing by taking that step is giving God a chance to show you that He really does love you and care about you and in a very personal way as a kind, caring Father. You are giving yourself a chance to experience that He is the best Dad in the whole world. He's also the most supportive Father you could ever hope for, one who can always be depended on to keep the promise that "He will never leave you. He will never abandon you." Hebrews 13:5 NLT

He's just like the Dad in this true Story

In 1989, an 8.2 earthquake almost flattened Armenia, killing over 30,000 people in less than four minutes. In the midst of utter devastation and chaos, a father left his wife securely at home and rushed to the school where his son was supposed to be. That's when he discovered that the building was as flat as a pancake.

After the traumatic initial shock, he remembered the promise he had made to his son: "No matter what, I'll always be there for you!"

Tears began to fill his eyes. As he looked at the pile of debris that once was the school, it looked hopeless, but he kept remembering his commitment to his son. He began to concentrate on where he walked his son to class at school each morning. Remembering that his son's classroom would be in the back right corner of the building, he rushed there and started digging through the rubble.

As he was digging, other forlorn parents arrived, clutching their hearts, saying: "My son!" "My daughter!"

Other well-meaning parents tried to pull him off of what was left of the school saying:

 "It's too late!"

"They're dead!"

"You can't help!"

"Go home!"

"Come on, face reality, there's nothing you can do! You're just going to make things worse!"

To each parent he responded with one line: "Are you going to help me now?"

Then he proceeded to dig for his son, stone by stone.

Soon the fire chief showed up and tried to pull him off of the school's debris. He told this father, "Fires are breaking out, explosions are everywhere. You are in danger. We'll take care of it. Go home."

To which this loving, caring Armenian father asked, "Are you going to help me now?"

The police came and said, "You're angry, distraught and it's over. You're endangering others. Go home. We'll handle it!"

To which he replied, "Are you going to help me now?"

No one helped.

Courageously he proceeded alone. He needed to know for himself: "Is my boy alive or is he dead?"

He kept digging.

In the thirty-eighth hour, he pulled back a boulder and heard his son's voice. He screamed his son's name, "Armand!"

He heard back, "Dad!?"

"It's me, Dad!" the boy cried out. "I told the other kids not to worry. If you were alive, you'd save me. And when you saved me, they'd be saved. You promised me that no matter what, you'll always be there for me! And you did it, Dad!"

"What's going on in there? How is it?" the father asked.

"There are fourteen of us left out of thirty-three, Dad. We're scared, hungry, thirsty and thankful you're here. When the building collapsed, it made a wedge, like a triangle, and that saved us."

"Come on out, boy!"

"No, Dad! Let the other kids out first, because I know you'll get me! No matter what, I know you'll be there for me!"

Taken from "Chicken Soup for the Soul"
1999 Father's Day Message

God longs to be that kind of Dad to each His children. Yet once again, if letting Him have this kind of relationship with you is a struggle, this was my "not so great" attitude when I was saved:

"Jesus is my Savior. I love Him.
But I want nothing to do with God as my Father.
That I have no interest in at all."

Those were tragic years in my life when "father" was one of the ugliest words in the English language.

Yet I had no clue that my feeling this way deeply saddened Jesus because the Father meant everything to Him. When I saw this, I was so sorry that I decided to let God have a chance.

That's the moment when I experienced a comfort I'd never known before.

His kindness began to melt the walls around my heart. It was the beginning of God becoming the first **real** Father I'd ever known.

Then He told me: "You have not received a spirit of slavery leading to fear again. You have received a spirit of adoption, by which you may cry out to Me, 'Abba Father.'" Romans 8:15 NASB

I was amazed that in the Greek, "Abba Father" is as personal and intimate a name as if we were saying to Him "Papa God" or "dear Daddy."

> **This very personal relationship with the Father is what you and I need because He does have a "plan for us, for good and not destruction, to give us a future and a hope."**
>
> **Yet we are seriously limited in being able to enter into all that He has for us if we feel sad and empty inside because we don't have Him as our Dad to help us.**

Putting the past behind us

Along this Journey of growing in a very personal relationship with the Father, I've realized that overcoming the pain caused by a hurtful past is **not** found in "stuffing" it, ignoring it, or minimizing what affected us.

What helps us become whole and then move on into everything God has planned for us is being fully honest with **ourselves** about how we are hurting, and be ***just as real*** with the Father about it also.

I found this freeing insight in the life of David.

He was cruelly rejected by his father, as if he didn't exist. He was publicly degraded by his brother, Eliab who spoke demeaning words to him in front of others. His friend, Saul betrayed him and viciously turned on him. He had many men killed in battle so that David could take the wife of one of those men. He also made serious mistakes with his children that caused him more and more heartache the older they got. So there was in many ways overwhelming pain in David that he had to face and overcome.

But what I find remarkable is how he didn't hide any of his feelings from himself or from God. Rather He faced them honestly.

He even said these pretty surprising things to God:

"Lord, why do You stand so far away?

Why do You hide when I need You the most? How long will You forget me? How long will You look the other way? How long must I struggle with anguish in my soul and sorrow in my heart every day?

My God, my God, why have You forsaken me? Why do You remain so distant? Why do You ignore my cries for help? Why have You tossed me aside?"

Psalm 10:1, 13:1-2, 22:1-2, 43:2 NLT

It's also amazing to me that God never scolded David for saying any of that to Him.

He was never upset about the blunt honesty.

He knew it would help David feel closer to Him.

So in response, the Father was only there for His son. He only treated this broken, hurting man with compassionate understanding. Then **after** his serious failures, God still called David a "man after His own heart" and he fulfilled his destiny as King.

Yet for some people, what's affecting them is so unclear that they can't be honest with themselves and with God like David was.

They need help seeing what is troubling them before they can do this and Word-based counseling can be the Father's merciful provision so that He can help them to be set free.

However what saddens me is I've known countless men and women who have received this help. But they **don't stop** analyzing their pain. Instead they continue talking and thinking about the hurts.

Those I've known who decided to go this direction as a way to cope with their past are just about all still stuck there. The years have gone by and they've never been able to put it all behind them and begin to live.

They also have become increasingly more self-focused because so much of their time is centered on thinking about themselves and their efforts to get healed from their hurts. It may even seem to them that this doing all this is wise, even helpful.

But it's a quest that seriously hinders their ability to have the rewarding relationships the Father wants for them to experience in the present. Because these mutually healthy relationships are not possible when someone gets caught up in putting way too much energy, time and effort into thinking about themselves in an endless attempt to "fix" their lives.

This self-focus also shuts down intimacy with God because when they try to worship, often all they can see is themselves, their pain and what they need from Him. And He does very much care about our needs. But, when any believer turns his time of being with God into mainly thinking about himself and what He can do for him, this is a one-way, self-centered relationship.

Yet **no** relationship can be close if it's about one person thinking mainly about themselves, their needs and their struggles.

This will destroy closeness with **anyone**, including God.

Sometimes people keep looking at their past because they want to recall what they can't remember.

They think that's going to help their heart to heal. But in all my decades of ministry, including extensive pastoral counseling trying to help people understand what is troubling them that happened a long time ago, I've never known anyone who benefitted from trying to get their mind to remember what it does not recall.

Instead I've only seen this effort devour precious years of their life. Sadly, what a person is searching for, even if they don't realize it, is a way to regain what they've lost. But none of these efforts can ever give back to them the love they missed out on. Worse yet, trying to remember what the mind does not recall will cause what they do remember to become even more painfully raw.

Meanwhile, God's plan for them is shipwrecked. Living life to the fullest is on hold until all the endless levels of hurts are examined and the pain of the past is able to rob them all over again. Then, even if they start to do better, as soon as another hurt comes along or another troubling reminder of the past affects them, they often think they are not "healed." So they have to return to the analyzing and talk about these new hurts.

To be honest, I have many years of my childhood that I can't remember at all and I'm hugely grateful for those missing pieces in my memories.

I consider what I can't recall from my past a gift of mercy and kindness from God. I celebrate that He did this for me.

I also decided not to even try to remember any of it. I just wanted to face the pain of the past that I did very clearly remember and then put it all behind me so that I could move on with where God wanted to take me. This decision made it possible for me to pour my whole heart into what was ahead of me that a loving Father wanted me to enjoy living to the fullest for Him.

However, if I had gone the direction of trying to figure out every detail of my past, including trying to remember what I had no memory of, I'd still be working on it. None of this moving forward would have been possible.

So I'm overwhelmingly grateful that the Bible **doesn't** tell us to keep on trying to uncover every detail of our past hurts or keep on thinking and talking about them.

This is what a loving, kind Father tells us to focus on:

> "Let us run with endurance the race that God has set before us. We do this by keeping our eyes on Jesus on whom our faith depends from start to finish."
>
> Hebrews 12:1-2 NLT

But we **can't** keep our eyes on Jesus when we continue to focus on what is negative, such as our past. It's just not possible. Devastating experiences are that powerful in how they can keep our thoughts riveted on the losses in our life.

Yet when we honestly face our hurts, and we forgive, and decide "enough is enough" by refusing to think and talk about them, then we can enter into a whole new realm of freedom.

What's amazing is that in this new place where the past no longer has the power to rob us, what happened to us that caused us so much heartache can't control our lives anymore.

We also get to experience our loving Dad giving us a new beginning in His "future and hope" for us, just as He encourages us will happen in these deeply reassuring words:

The Father says, "Please come."

"Oh My beloved child, please come and be with Me whenever you are having a hard time.

I promise you as your very real Dad that each time you do, not only will you be in My presence where you will be helped in very encouraging ways, but how I long to be in **your** presence.

Whenever you come, for even just a moment at a time, I will comfort you as no one else can.

But as you do, I need for you to lay down all the thoughts of yourself, and all the thoughts of your pain and difficulties, and come to just be with Me.

Then as your Father who loves you more than you could ever hope for or imagine, I will come to be with you also. And in the places you are still hurting, I can heal you, and it won't take years and years. Instead, with each touch of My kind presence upon you, you can go miraculously from healing to healing.

Each time you come to be close to Me, I also promise I will refresh your weary, broken places so that when you turn and face your life again, you will be amazed. The circumstances may still be exactly the same. But everything will look different because you have experienced how understanding I am about how you are feeling.

So I say to you, please come often into My presence.

As you do, I will revive My destiny for you that you have been feeling so discouraged about, wondering if it will ever happen.

In that closeness with Me, you will be strengthened because I can show you what I'm doing in your life, your calling, your destiny, your work, your ministry.

As you enter into that most sacred place to just be with Me, I will anoint you afresh with my prophetic anointing. I will open up to you the secrets on My heart and reveal to you what I'm doing among My people, and for the hurting and lost of the nations.

As you bow your heart, your knees, your whole life before Me with humble, repentant brokenness and as you die to every mindset that is holding you back and defeating you, I am going to do a new thing in your life. My child, it's already begun.

So My child, when you awaken each morning, before you do anything else, please want to be with Me for just a moment. Then throughout each day, talk to Me as a dearest friend does with his dearest friend.

When you put your head on the pillow each night, fall asleep telling Me you love Me. But not in fancy words. Just in childlike, simple, from the heart, sincere words. And if you wake up in the night troubled, anxious, or afraid, instantly start talking to Me. Begin to think about My presence and wanting to be close to Me.

I will come to be with you. I will come in a heartbeat. You will feel safe and protected by My love for you.

You will be able to peacefully fall asleep in My sheltering presence.

To reassure you, I fully understand as your Dad that there will be bumps along the way. There will be mistakes.

That's why this Journey of you fulfilling My plan for your life is **not** about you being perfect.

I ***already know*** as your Father that there will be times when you will need My help to be restored to the fullness of all this because of the mistakes you make along the way.

All I ask of you is that you sincerely try and seek Me with a humble heart. Then, even when you have 'blown it' and you are struggling, you will still be one of My servants through whom I will show forth My glory, just like happened to David, and Peter, and Paul.

So please, stay close to Me, no matter what happens in your life and you will be one of My godly ones who will bless Me.

You will speak of the glory of My Kingdom and talk of My power. To make known to the sons of men My mighty acts and the glory of the majesty of My Kingdom."

- Your Father and your Dad

Psalm 145:10-12 NASB

Chapter Five

GOD UNDERSTANDS

A personal Awakening to Revival can also be sabotaged if we have the wrong idea about who God is whenever we are up against deeply painful times in our life.

This happened to me shortly after I was saved when I heard a lot of Christians saying:

> Whatever God wants
> always happens.
>
> Nothing takes place that
> He does not step back and allow.
>
> He has the power to
> stop anything He wants to stop.
>
> He also has a reason
> for everything that happens.

I didn't have any idea **what part** of this was true and what wasn't.

So a confusing perception of who God is began in my heart. As a result, I started to feel betrayed by Him.

I even began to say to Him with anger and a broken heart:

"Since this is who You are, **why** didn't You stop the abuse being done to me? Why didn't You intervene and protect me?

You are all powerful. So how can You say You love me, God and yet You just watched it? You just let it all happen?

Why didn't You stop what was being forced on my sister? You heard her terrified screams. She was frantic to escape what my parents were doing to her. But You did nothing to help her!

Why didn't You do something about the sexual things being done to my younger brother? It affected his mind so horribly that it drove him into mental illness and violence. He's never been normal.

How could You allow all this to happen to an innocent, helpless young boy? Joe was so special. And all this being done to him ruined his life."

Eventually I was set free from this tormenting confusion when I realized that "God cares about the anguish of our soul and in all our suffering, He also suffered." Psalm 31:7 NLT, Isaiah 63:9 NLT

This meant that every moment any of us were in pain as a child, God's heart was broken. He grieved that the parents He gave us so that they could love us would choose to do such terrible things to us. He longed to reach down and help us.

He ached to scoop us up into His arms to shelter us.

But He had to wait until we were willing to give Him a chance to be our Father. Only then could He pour His healing love into our broken heart.

Also because God loves us with such a tender caring, whenever He hears us asking why He didn't stop bad people from doing such terrible things to us when were so innocent and vulnerable, He **doesn't** get upset with us.

He understands how we feel. He hurts for us more than we can ever know. He aches to help us so that we don't distance ourselves from Him.

As I struggled to find peace in my own soul in this area of heartrending questions and troubling confusion that affects so many people, reflecting on this story helped me to find peace:

If a man decides to drive his car after he has had a lot of alcohol and he kills a five year old little girl, it wasn't her fault that she died.

It also wasn't God's fault.

He never wanted her innocent life to be snuffed out before she ever even had a chance to live. He never, ever wanted this man to use his free will to cause this tragedy.

All the Father could do was weep over the heartbreaking end to this child's life and grieve over the terrible heartache of her devastated parents.

What grieves God is that although He is all powerful and almighty and though He has the power to stop all bad things from happening, a long time ago when He created man, He sovereignly decided to give people free will so that they could freely choose to have a relationship with Him.

But He never wanted this precious gift to be used to hurt people. That's why when this happens, it breaks His heart. He also doesn't make the decision of free will one person or one moment at a time. So when a drunk kills someone while driving, it's not because God stepped back in that particular situation and decided not to intervene. The decision to give man free will was settled ages and ages ago when He created man.

Yet when my first dangerously abusive marriage ended and I foolishly rushed into another one, I still had a lot of confusion about who God is. I had no clue that He doesn't want to control us. He only encourages us to seek Him and be close to Him so that we will be able to make the right choices. He does warn us when we are going in the wrong direction, but only to protect us from doing the things that will end up hurting us. With the true heart of a caring Dad, He earnestly wants to help us have a fulfilling, rewarding life.

But I didn't see all this when I was a young believer.

I only knew I had begged God to protect me from marrying the wrong person again. So I was horrified when I discovered on our honeymoon that this man was far more cruel in his abuse than my first husband.

As time went on, and my children and I suffered horrifically, I felt the Father had betrayed me. I angrily told Him:

"I trusted You! Why did You allow this to happen to me? I told You I only wanted Your will. **Why** didn't You warn me? You are all powerful. Why didn't You stop me?"

Only years later did I grasp that God **did** warn me many times when I was dating this man that I needed to end my involvement with him.

But I chose not to listen.

He even sent a trusted friend into my life who told me: "I guarantee if you marry him, you will regret it." Yet I refused to slow down and at least consider if the Father was trying to protect me, and my children, from another serious mistake. Consequently, we lived fourteen more years in a nightmare of the worst kinds of brutally scarring, heartbreaking, degrading abuse.

My husband, Barry describes how he was affected by this same area of troubling confusion about God and His sovereignty:

"From the time I started going to church at the age of twelve, I never heard the fact that He gave man free will. Therefore people can make choices that God doesn't want at all. Instead, I learned a very warped concept about the sovereignty of God. I was taught that He either causes or allows everything that happens. But believing this meant that everything that happened to me was His will. This mindset caused me a tremendous amount of pain and over the years I built up a lot of anger at Him for the disappointments and painful things in my life.

I felt that God didn't care if I suffered.

I also was troubled with the question, "Why doesn't He fix or stop the things that hurt me?"

For example, I married when I was nineteen and after fourteen years, I lost my family. No matter how much I prayed and asked God to restore my kids to a relationship with me, it didn't happen.

After a few years without receiving the answer that I expected, I was angry with God for not doing something to change the situation. I often told Him with a broken heart: 'For years I've prayed for my relationship with my kids to be restored and it hasn't happened. Why haven't You answered my prayers?'

This continuing, painful situation began to build up inside me and make me very angry at God. The worst one of all was that my children didn't change toward me. Because I prayed so much about this, I thought God didn't really care about me.

Boy, is that a bad place to be in!

Here Ruth and I were working in the ministry full time and I was angry at God. This was holding us back in what we were called to do together. It also began to affect our relationship because I could be very moody and difficult to be around. Finally, God used Ruth to help me understand what was wrong in my thinking.

One day when I was venting about Him not fixing the relationships with my kids, she looked at me and said:

'God is sovereign. But He decided at the beginning of creation to not control our choices. So He won't make your kids want to know you. If you don't learn this about God, it's going to ruin everything we have!'

That got my attention. I had learned the hard way about love and I love Ruth with my very life. So it didn't take me long to realize I was demanding that God would make my children love me again.

He doesn't make me do things and He won't make others do what I want. He doesn't even make us love Him, though that closeness to Him is what He longs for. Yet, it's only love when we choose to give it.

When I saw all this, the anger broke off me. I stopped blaming God for the choices of other people that He can't change. I also stopped asking Him to make my children do what I wanted them to do. Instead I prayed that He would find a way to help them want to know me.

But I still have to make sure the old way of thinking doesn't creep back into me. All the pain can instantly affect me again if I let myself focus on the loss of close relationship with my children.

So when those thoughts come at me, I now force myself to remember the lessons I've learned about love and choices and who God is and I have peace again."

Barry Johnson

Though the Father won't make anyone decide to do the right thing, I've learned we can pray that He will send people or circumstances into someone's life to help them see what God longs for them to understand.

Many times after I've prayed this way, I've witnessed someone deciding to go a different direction in their life.

Not always though.

But at least when God's efforts to reach someone don't work because they are not willing to see or listen, it's comforting to know we did pray and He did try to reach that person.

Then the rest is up to them and their freedom to make choices.

The Unexplainable

There will always be many things we can never understand.

If we try to figure out those unexplainable "whys," it will only cause us pain.

It can put us in the awful place of misunderstanding God and not wanting to be close to Him.

This is an example of the "unexplainable."

One night Barry and I were asked to minister to a twenty-four year old young man who was dying of an aggressive cancer. The doctors had given up on being able to help him. They had sent him home to die. When we arrived at his home, it was heartbreaking to watch him hobble down the hall in front of me while He leaned heavily on a crutch because he had already lost a leg and hip to the cancer. While I sat down across from him, he told me:

> "I want to live. I trusted God to heal me and then I lost my leg. So it's hard to believe in healing again. But I'm willing to trust Him one more time for a miracle."

I cried with him. The pained look in his eyes was heartrending. As I played my harp and heaven descended into that room, I wept over this young life that was being destroyed by cancer.

"For the rest of my life I will never forget you," I said as I hugged him goodbye. "Thank you. All I can say is thank you," he responded as he returned my hug.

Then I turned away from him, walked down the steps of the wooden porch and began to sob.

This special young man loved God so much. He wanted with everything in him to live to be an old man and experience life, love and family to the fullest. He ached for God to heal him and not let him die.

Barry and I, the family and many other believers kept passionately praying that the Father would supernaturally intervene. We cried out night and day that He would have mercy and miraculously deliver this young man from his death sentence. But the very aggressive cancer progressed. In just a couple of weeks he was gone.

In the midst of the overwhelming loss, there is no way we can **ever** figure out why he died, when so many trusted God to heal him.

We've known people He did sovereignly, supernaturally heal who also wanted with all their heart to live. So we can't ever understand why this miracle didn't happen for a young person who had such an exceptionally tender heart and was so full of love for God. It's just not possible for us to ever figure out why terrible things like this happen.

That's why whenever someone has asked me to explain, I can only respond:

"I don't know why."

Although there's so much we can't comprehend about God and tragic, unexplainable losses, this topic can't be ignored. The confusion about it is hurting far too many people. Often this is causing them to decide they don't want anything to do with being close to God. It just hurts too much. This includes many sincere Christians.

To be completely honest, this section was very hard for me to write because it is talking about a place of such terrible pain for so many people.

But gratefully, this is a comforting glimpse into God's caring heart toward those who are hurting because of unexplainable loss:

"Oh My child, I compassionately understand why you are upset with Me when something devastating hurts someone you love and you feel I let you down because I didn't stop it from happening.

How I wish that none of My children had to hurt with such terrible heartaches, diseases and griefs.

None of this is what I ever wanted.

This suffering is never what I planned when I gave Adam and Eve the gift of life and free will.

When I first created mankind, this is not the kind of world, at all, that I wanted any son or daughter of Mine to live in.

Yet because in the Garden man used My gift of free will to sin against Me, all mankind has suffered. Since then everyone has lived in a fallen, broken world where there is disease and death.

This sadly includes My own children, and the young and most innocent who never had a chance to live.

How I grieve and weep with a broken heart over those who are crushed by these devastating and confusing hurts. Yet when they blame Me for letting them down, I do understand their anger and confusion.

My heart only hurts for them and I never stop longing for the day they realize it was never My will or My plan that those who trust in Me would have to suffer all this grief and loss.

How I also want you to know that whenever you are hurting in this troubled, broken world, I'm here for you.

I want with all that I am as your Father to hold you close to Me during any of your moments of heartache and painfully troubling confusion about something that has happened to you or someone you dearly loved.

I yearn to reassure you any time you need to pour out all the pain in your heart about what's hard on you.

So please be honest with Me about all you are feeling. I want to do all I can possibly do to comfort you.

How I hope that what I've shared with you as your Dad can help you feel closer to Me.

How I ache for you to know that in all your tears, I cry, too. I weep as a Father would weep over His child who is in terrible pain. What breaks your heart, breaks Mine.

I'm affected more than you could ever begin to imagine by your grief and I long to have you come close to Me so that I can heal the broken places in your heart.

Please also know that night and day, I'm here for you. I'm here with wide open arms to help you and reassure you that I do understand."

- Your Father and your Dad

Chapter Six

THE PATH TO OUR DESTINY

At fourteen, I already felt so lost that I thought a lot about how to find meaning for my life. That's when I discovered this poem that throughout my life has been an ongoing source of inspiration for me.

The Road Less Taken
By Robert Frost
Adapted and Personalized

Two roads diverged in a yellow wood,
and yet I could not travel both
and be one traveler.

Long I stood and looked down
one as far as I could.

Then took the other because
it was grassy and wanted wear.
Both that morning lay in leaves
no step had trodden black.

I kept the first for another day.
Yet knowing how way leads on to way,
I knew I would never come back.

I shall be telling this story
somewhere ages and ages hence.

Two roads diverged in a wood.
And I, I took the one less traveled by.
And that has made all the difference.

When people don't find this path that gives them a sense of meaningful purpose, life becomes increasingly more void of anything worth living for. This is how I overcame feeling that way.

***

The world and sometimes even the Body of Christ are impressed by people with wealth, fame, beauty, popularity and high levels of education and accomplishment.

Yet these are **not** the criteria God uses when He chooses people to be used by Him. He isn't looking for flashy, charismatic, powerfully gifted, highly accomplished people to do His mighty works.

Down through history, God has used simple, ordinary women, men, and young people who had a humble, passionate longing to be close to Him and were willing to do whatever He asked of them.

In these words, the Father lets us know that He **isn't** looking for those He can use who are important in the eyes of people:

"God chose things the world considers foolish in order to shame those who think they are wise. And He chose things that are powerless to shame those who are powerful."
1 Corinthians 1:27 NLT

This quote by Frank Bartleman, the eyewitness historian of the Azusa Street Revival, captures this same perspective:

> "The Lord's heroes will arise from the dust of obscure and despised circumstances. He draws from the deepest seclusion the weak instruments by which He purposes to accomplish great things. For this reason, most of those God used to set the world on fire through the Azusa Street Revival came from this obscurity."
> *Frank Bartleman*

One of those "heroes" was William Seymour.

He was a poor, one-eyed black man with a severely scarred face. He was uneducated and totally unknown. He also was constantly up against the rejection that was part of being physically deformed and black in that era. Yet this was the man God chose to be the Apostle of this Revival.

Another unlikely person was Smith Wigglesworth.

He was an uneducated plumber who couldn't even read. Nonetheless he became an Evangelist who was powerfully used by God.

Amos was another ordinary man.

Yet God used him as a prophet to Israel. Amos even said about himself: "I'm not one of your professional prophets. I certainly never trained to be one. I'm just a shepherd and I take care of fig trees. But the Lord called me away from my flock and told me, 'Go prophesy to my people in Israel.'" Amos 7:14-15 NLT

Next comes Gideon.

The Midianites were so brutal that the Israelites fled to the mountains. God called Gideon to deliver them. However, when He told Gideon how He wanted to use him, this was his insecure response: "How can I save Israel? My family is the poorest in the whole Tribe of Manasseh. And I am the least thought of in the entire family." Judges 6:15 TLB   But even though he was this down on himself and although he felt completely useless in the eyes of others, hidden inside of Gideon was someone the Father wanted to use. So He looked past all the insecurity of this man who was so beat up by life, and said to him what He says to us if that is how we ever feel: "Mighty hero! The Lord is with you!"

And there's David.

When the Prophet Samuel asked his father, Jesse to bring his sons to him, he didn't include David with his brothers. Only after the Prophet questioned, "Are these all the sons you have?" did Jesse mention his youngest one who was taking care of the sheep. Even after he was publicly anointed to be king by a highly respected prophet, his own brother, Eliab demeaned him in front of other people. This occurred when David asked questions about Goliath and Eliab cruelly responded: "What are you doing around here anyway? What about those few sheep you're supposed to be taking care of? I know about your pride and dishonesty. You just want to see the battle." 1 Samuel 17:28 NLT

What he was actually saying to David was: "Who do you think you are, David? You will never amount to anything. Just go back and do what you always do. Stop thinking you can do anything that matters at all with your life."

Yet this overlooked teenager was the one God "selected from the common people to be king." Psalm 89:19 NLT And even though no one else thought his life was worth anything at all, God saw David with very different eyes. That's what He does for each of us, no matter what negative, unkind words others may say to us.

Then came Jesus.

He could have been born into an elite family of great influence. He actually could have come as royalty and lived in an exquisitely beautiful palace, surrounded by extravagant comfort. Instead, Jesus chose to come into this world in a humble stable. A darkened barn filled with the smell of sheep, camels, cows and donkeys. There was only a dirt floor to lie down on and there was no way to fill it with welcoming light or warmth. He grew up among the common people.

As a young man, He preferred to spend time with the lowly and humble, rather than be with those who considered themselves important. He definitely didn't try to hang out with anyone just so that they could help Him build a big ministry someday. He also could have picked the most educated, gifted, articulate, accomplished, "important" people of His time to help Him set in motion His plan to evangelize the world.

But Jesus *didn't* do this!

He chose uneducated, simple people whom others saw as so insignificant that this is what they said about them:

"The members of the council were amazed when they saw the boldness of Peter and John. For they could see that they were **ordinary** men who had no special training." Acts 4:13 NLT

This description of Jesus powerfully captures the humbleness of His life and ministry:

He was born in an obscure village.

He grew up as the child of a peasant woman.

He worked in a carpenter shop until He was thirty.

For three years, He was an itinerant preacher.

He never wrote a book.

He never held an office.

He never had a family or owned a home.

He didn't go to college.

He never visited a big city.

He never traveled two hundred miles from the place where He was born.

Jesus did none of the things that usually accompany greatness.

Yet, He shook the world at its very foundation and became the Savior of us all. *Author Unknown*

I'm so thankful that Jesus decided to live this way and that He chose to use "unimportant" people to serve the Father with Him. This inspires hope that God can still use ordinary women, men and young people, and in far reaching ways.

I am someone who needed this hope.

My family lived in the slums of South Boston across from a soot-blackened factory and a rat and cockroach infested bus barn. Our home was a cramped tenement with only cold water and no heat except from a coal burning stove. Each day I lived in dread of my encounters with large rats and swarms of huge cockroaches that I ran away from. When I was six, we moved to California and lived behind an old donut shop. The only way to our front door was past a row of beat up garbage cans. They were always stuffed with rotting garbage that reeked with a nauseating smell. To make matters worse, I cringed as I stepped over the maggots that were everywhere. I was so mortified by the thought of anyone seeing where I lived that I never invited anyone to come to our home.

The years when we lived in the Projects were even worse.

But shortly before I graduated from eighth grade, my older brother was very concerned about what was happening to me. He petitioned the nuns of an exclusive Notre Dame Academy to give me a chance to succeed in their school and I was given a full scholarship. Then every day I gratefully boarded the bus that took me across the railroad tracks and far away from the Projects. However, I dreaded the days when we didn't have to wear uniforms because the other girls came from wealthy families. They had beautiful clothes and mine were old and shabby. This was so humiliating for me as a teenager that I withdrew even more into my own world, where no one could get close to me.

At eighteen I entered the convent. As a Catholic nun, I taught second grade. But I never graduated from college.

When I left after five years, I could only get minimum-wage employment.

I married a year later. But it was a horrifically abusive, violent, even life-threatening relationship that ended after seven years. At that point, I was destitute. I had two young children to raise by myself, with no help or support from anyone.

I was completely alone.

Yet one day God looked beyond all this and told me these amazing words. He's speaking them to anyone who feels that their life is not of much value at all.

"My child, go for it!

Step out of where you are and begin to live the life I have destined and planned for you.

As you do, please remember young David. I took him from a lowly, hidden away place where no one thought he would amount to anything and I raised him up to be king. I did that for him even though he failed in many ways.

His failures could not stop My plan for him because I saw the sincere humbleness of his heart.

THE PATH TO OUR DESTINY

So I promise you that if you will sincerely try to love Me and to live by what My Word shows you to do, then I will do the same for you as I did for young David.

I will use you far beyond what others, or even yourself, have ever thought possible.

I also urge you to lay down all the limitations you've put on yourself and those that others have put on you. I ache for you to stop thinking about the cruel, discouraging words others have said to you. Those mean words will only continue to hurt you. If you keep thinking about them, they could even destroy you and all I have planned for you to live and experience that will bring you such joy.

To help you, I have words of hope and life to tell you about yourself. And My words can radically change the whole direction of your life!

I also want you to know, deep in your heart, that I do understand all the times you've felt like a useless, invisible, meaningless outsider when you've been with other people.

But none of that is how I see you!

So please, take My hand and step out of the darkness you have felt.

As you do, you will discover new hope and so much encouragement about what I've destined for your life.

You will be comforted by spending simple times with Me, talking to Me honestly about all that's in your heart.

And I will show you the way to a completely different path for your life, a path you couldn't even see before. But as your Dad, I see it and I know how to help you find your way there and how to give you the courage to walk along it.

I long to be able to help you begin living the life I planned for you before you were even born.

So please come.

Always I care about you more than you could ever even imagine."

- Your Father and your Dad

1 Samuel 13:14, 17:7 NASB
1 Kings 3:6 NLT
Acts 13:22 NLT
Isaiah 41:13 NASB
Hebrews 13:5 NASB
Galatians 4:6 NLT
Psalm 103:14 NLT

Chapter Seven

FREEDOM

Another issue that can stop us from experiencing the fullness of God's destiny for us is our negative thoughts toward ourselves. The Father used this story to help me see how easily this can happen. It also opened my eyes to how I ended up stuck in defeat because of the unhealthy ways I was thinking, and how I could get out of that ditch and never go back.

The Eagle and the Chicken

"One day a farmer found an eagle's egg and, thinking it was one of his chicken's eggs, placed it in a nest in his chicken coop. The egg hatched and the baby eagle grew up thinking that he was a chicken. The eagle did what the chickens did. It scratched the dirt for seeds and worms. It did not fly more than a few feet because this is what chickens did.

One day he saw an eagle flying gracefully and majestically in the open sky. He asked a chicken friend 'What is that beautiful bird?'

The chicken said 'That is an eagle. He is an outstanding bird, but you can't fly like him because you are just a chicken.' So the eagle never gave a second thought to it and lived and died as a chicken." *Randy Pottenger*

When I read that story the first time, I thought to myself:

"What a tragedy. He was built to soar into the heavens. Yet conditioned to stay earthbound, he pecked at stray seeds and chased insects. Though destined to be among the most awesome of all birds, instead he believed his neighbor's counsel and the lies he accepted about himself. He never understood that he could have joined those majestic birds in the sky and soared with them like an eagle."

But the Father interrupted my thoughts and really surprised me when He showed me:

"That's how you've been looking at life, even though I have so much more for you to experience and discover."

In that illuminating moment I realized that although the Father wants to use simple, ordinary people for His amazing purposes, we'll never be able to experience it as long as we keep thinking like someone who is living in a chicken coop. Yet what's sad is we were created and destined to live, and think like the eagle.

But so many sincere Christians never experience all they could become.

I encounter them everywhere I go and I feel such compassion for them because I vividly remember when I felt just as lost and empty as they still feel.

That's why I'll never forget the grief I was overwhelmed by when I was the Secretary of an Alternative High School. One morning I was looking out the window of a storage room. Far above me, soaring in the sky was a large, magnificent bird. Tears instantly streamed down my cheeks as I stifled a sob and told God:

"I ache to fly free. I long to be set free from feeling so painfully lost. My heart feels crushed by sadness and despair because I feel so far away from what I thought my life was going to be all about. Please help me. Please set me free."

When I said this desperate prayer, I had no idea that I was putting on God all the responsibility for change in my life. Yet He was actually waiting for *me* to make certain choices so that He could help me to live free. Eventually I had to face that I was drowning emotionally in paralyzing discouragement because of all the wrong paths I had chosen my entire life. As a result, I couldn't handle the thought of taking the risk of trying something that might not work out. But there came a day when this destructive way of thinking was turned upside down and the whole direction of my life changed.

This is what happened.

In 1997, my husband, Barry and I said yes to the Lord and laid down everything we had to serve Him.

Immediately I felt stretched in my willingness to trust Him.

This uncomfortable feeling actually started for me when God showed Barry He wanted us to move from San Diego, California to Seattle, Washington to birth a church. Barry was eager to leave. He was born in Portland and had longed to return to the Northwest for many years. But we knew absolutely no one there and Barry had no job where he felt God was calling us to go.

The thought of all this happening was distressing for me because my roots were entrenched in California. This is where I had raised a family, established friendships and built a fruitful ministry. I didn't want to leave all that I had known for most of my life.

Even more painful for me to consider, if we left San Diego I would be moving away from my adult children. This meant giving up the family dinners and holidays together that I had dreamed about since I had been a young mother. Losing all this grieved me. These hopes and dreams were such an important part of my life that I didn't want to give all this up. While I wrestled with an overwhelming feeling of loss every time I thought about moving far away from California, the Father shocked me. One morning this is how He showed me that my way of thinking was a huge mistake:

"My glory cloud over you and Barry has moved to the Northwest. Will you go where I am going or will you choose to stay where you are comfortable?

It is true that if you decide to remain here, you will have a good life. I will still love you and take care of you.

But you and Barry will miss out on My very best for you. If you cling to what is familiar and take the path that is comfortable, My purposes for you will be frustrated. In the years ahead, you will have a deadness and emptiness in your soul. Because the fulfillment of My promises for you will not happen here. They can only come to pass in the new place where I'm asking you to go."

This was all very sobering. So I told the Father I would go. Within a year we packed up all of our belongings. But all the way from California to Seattle, tears rolled down my cheeks, while I stared out the window of the U-Haul truck and watched the miles race by. With a broken heart I chose to obey God and put behind me all that had ever given meaning to my life. I mourned that I was saying goodbye to the only place I had ever found a home for my heart and where I finally felt I belonged. I also grieved over the loss of not being with my adult children the way I had always dreamed and hoped for.

Yet it was in the Northwest where we found the family and priceless friendships that God planned for us to experience. They each surpass every relationship either of us had ever known. I shudder every time I think about what we would have never experienced if I had refused to leave California. Nonetheless, for the longest time tears came easily whenever I experienced a painful sense of loss.

Those tears still happen. Quite honestly, I will always miss what I lost.

One day in the midst of this struggle, a friend unexpectedly sent me this story:

> "A young girl traveling on a train for the first time heard that it would have to cross several rivers. She was troubled and fearful as she thought of the water. But each time the train came to a river, a bridge was always there to provide a safe way across. After passing safely over several rivers and streams, the girl settled back in her seat with a sigh of relief and said to her mother, 'I'm not worried anymore. Somebody has put bridges for us all of the way.'" *Corrie Ten Boom*

Then the Father gave me this message. It is for anyone who needs His reassurance.

> "I will be for you that bridge over troubled waters so that you also can find your way to the other side.
>
> Every time you are in a place where you need that miracle to get to a place of safety, I will be there.
>
> I will make the impossible, possible.
>
> I will do the same for you as I did for that young child on the train. I will provide an unexpected bridge for you whenever you need for Me to do that for you.

I will do this so that you can walk over it to a place of safety and fully enter into the life I long for you to have as My beloved child."

- Your Father and your very real Dad

Many times since that day I've marveled when God did provide an unexpected bridge that I could walk over to a place of safety.

I just didn't know it was there.

Yet, despite all that I was learning and experiencing that meant so much to me, for several years I still didn't let anyone all the way into my heart. I had decided a long time ago not to trust. This stopped me benefitting from what it had taken a lifetime to understand about relationships. Nonetheless, closeness to people didn't feel safe. I felt this way even though:

> "All along there was the hope in my heart that I
> would be set free to experience the freedom I yearned for."
> Romans 8:20-21 NCV

These are the insights God showed me that challenged me to stop allowing my old ways of looking at life to defeat me:

Life hurts.

People hurt.

This happens in the chicken coup with others who never can understand us because they are not kindred with us. But the hurts also happen when we are flying free.

So I might as well get hurt being healthy, and give a few people a chance to get close to me.

That's when the kind of relationships I had yearned for since I was a little girl began to happen.

I also discovered that even God tells us:

"We belong to each other.
Each of us needs all the others."
Romans 12:4-5 NLT

Then when we are battered by the storms of life, we are not facing them alone. We can find strength and courage by staying close to those the Father gives us to share our lives with. This description of Redwood Trees powerfully captures this new way of thinking that transformed my life:

If these grandest, most majestic of trees are alone in the forest, they don't make it. They have a very large, but shallow root system. When a really bad storm comes along, they are easily uprooted and crash to the ground. But when they grow close to other Redwoods, they hang on to each other's roots. Then in the fiercest of storms they continue to stand tall and strong.

Paul the Apostle was definitely honest about him having this same need for supportive relationships: "I'm eager to encourage you in your faith, but I also want to be encouraged by yours. In this way, each of us will be a blessing to the other." Romans 1:12 NLT

But most of all, I marvel that **even Jesus** didn't want to be alone during His hard times. He made this very clear when He said to His disciples: "You have stayed with Me through My struggles." Luke 22:28 NCV

He also made it a high priority to have time with those closest to Him so that He didn't face whatever He was up against with only the Father being there for Him.

These are eye-opening glimpses into His need for others to be close to Him:

> "Jesus took Peter, James, and John to the top of the Mountain. No one else was there. At another time, He stopped the crowd. He wouldn't let anyone go with Him except Peter, James and John. And one day, when the apostles returned, they told Jesus everything they had done. Then He took them with Him to a town where they could be alone."
>
> Mark 9:2, 5:37, Luke 9:10 NLT

This means that the longer we walk with God, and the more passionately we embrace what He wants us to do for Him, the more we need trusted, kindred people to walk through life with us.

We don't outgrow this need.

We don't get so strong and mature that the Father wants to be our only close Friend and our only source of encouragement, help and support.

Jesus and Paul certainly didn't live that way.

Therefore, the longer we give our lives to the Father's purpose for us, the more significantly we need a few who can be a safe home and a comforting refuge for our heart.

Yet when I was a young Christian I made it very difficult for these destiny relationships to happen for me because I completely misunderstood the Prophet Isaiah when he wrote:

> "They that wait upon the Lord shall renew their strength.
> They shall mount up with wings as eagles."
> Isaiah 40:31 KJV

I thought this verse meant waiting for God to use me. Consequently, I was always looking for something big, off in the future, that some day was going to happen. I couldn't see or value what the Father wanted me to enter into each and every day for Him in the present. As a result, I missed out on encountering the people He had destined for me to know. So I was stunned when I first noticed this blunt statement that didn't line up at all with the way I had interpreted Isaiah:

> "If you wait for perfect conditions,
> you will never get anything done."
> Ecclesiastes 11:4 NLT

Eventually I also discovered that the Hebrew for the word "wait" in Isaiah 40:31 meant to trust God confidently and hope strongly. It had nothing to do with putting life on hold while waiting for something to happen someday. That's when I realized how much I had hindered myself from experiencing the close relationships from the Father that I was meant to walk through life with.

I also saw how my wrong thinking about "waiting" had crippled me being able to fully step into the fullness of His plan for my life.

When I first saw all this, it hit me:

Life is not a dress rehearsal.

Once today is over, it's gone forever.

It's not coming back.

That's also when these quotes that I had collected through the years began to mean a whole lot more to me:

"At the end of life, it won't matter what kind of house we own, or even if we own a home. It won't matter what kind of car we have or how many clothes we possess. It won't even matter how much we have in the bank. All that will matter are the faces that come to mind of those the Father sent into our lives so that we could bring to them His kindness and the hopeful safety of His humble, simple love." *Author Unknown*

"Sometimes we don't recognize the significance of the moments in our lives. We think that moment will come again and it will be there for another day. But we don't realize that day will not be coming back. We will pass that way only once. So if there is any kindness I can show or any good thing I can do, I need to do it now. I will not pass this way again." *Etienne De Grellet, Nathan Scott*

We also don't have to wait until our lives are "fixed" for God to use us. Yet everywhere the Father sends us to minister, my husband, Barry and I encounter sincere Christians who are disheartened by believing that they have to have everything going right in their personal lives before God can use them. But that mindset doesn't line up at all with what happened to David. Although his personal life was an extreme mess, the Father powerfully used him and in ways that are still profoundly affecting generations. He certainly never said to David: "First get your personal life all straightened out and then I can use you in My calling and plan for you."

There is such freedom in seeing life from this perspective. We don't have to wait any longer for God to use us.

Every single day it is possible for destiny and "redwood tree" relationships to happen.

But it takes courage to live like this.

It's rewarding. Yet it isn't easy.

Consequently I've often found encouragement in thinking about the truths in these quotes:

"Twenty years from now you will be more disappointed by the things you didn't try than by the ones you did do. So throw off the bowlines. Sail away from the safe harbor. Catch the trade winds in your sails. Explore. Dream. Discover." *Twain*

"Far better it is to dare mighty things, to win glorious triumphs, even though checkered by failure, than to rank with those poor spirits who neither enjoy nor suffer much because they live in the gray twilight that knows neither victory nor defeat." *Roosevelt*

"Success is never final. Failure is never fatal. It is courage that counts." *Churchill*

"I would rather attempt to do something great and fail, than attempt to do nothing, and succeed. Our greatest glory does not consist in never failing, but in rising every time we fall." *Schuller*

"A survey was done in a convalescent hospital for the elderly who were so ill they would never be going back home again. They were asked what they wish they had done differently as they look back over their lives. Many of them said: 'I wish I had taken more risks. Then at the end of my life, when it's too late to do anything about it, I wouldn't be feeling so sad that I didn't try the new things I wanted to do. Instead I limited myself by not taking risks that may not work out. All this regret is such a discouraging way to feel as I look back on my life.'" *Author Unknown*

To help people see how they can avoid missing out on living life to the fullest, I compiled a list of mindsets that can cause that sad loss to happen. There's also a second list of the courageous choices made by someone who has decided to live and think like an eagle.

Chicken Coop Thinking

I've failed so much and I've made so many wrong choices that the thought of even trying the things God wants to do feels like way too much.

I've blown it so much that I don't feel worthy of being loved anymore.

I feel so guilty about things I've done that I don't see how God can use me in any way that matters much at all.

I feel so broken by all the times I "missed it" that I'm devastated by feeling inadequate, insecure, confused and completely discouraged. Feeling this way has brought on me such a paralysis emotionally that I can't believe anymore that any of this can change.

I've been hurt so much that it's too scary to trust anyone again. It's too frightening to let anyone all the way into my heart. So I won't, even though I feel lonely and isolated. Because if I get close to people, I could get hurt again. I'm going to play it safe. I'm going to do all I can to not let anyone have the chance to hurt me again.

FREEDOM

My life is a mess because of what others did to me as a child. I have to first understand all the hurts in my past and figure them all out before I think about God using me.

What He wants me to do with my life has to be on hold until I finish working on all this really painful stuff from my past.

I've been working on forgiving for years.

But I just don't have any feelings to be able to do that. I know that the forgiving won't be the "real deal" if I don't feel it.

And finding a way to get completely over my past has to happen before I can get on with my life and really give myself to God's plan for me.

God is in complete control of everything that happens in my life. So I'm waiting for Him to change my circumstances and I'm waiting for Him to change me.

I wish my life could matter.

I wish I could make a difference.

But I have too much that needs to happen and be in place before I can try living like that.

I need to keep waiting for God to use me in a big and important way before I can actually fulfill His plan for me. Since that big thing hasn't happened yet, I'll just keep waiting for what my life is all about to take place.

No one in my family thinks I'll ever amount to anything. I think they are right. No one believes in me. So why bother trying.

I'm just an ordinary person. I don't see how God could use someone like me.

I'm too old to be thinking about hopes and dreams. My time for God using me is over. It's too late for that to happen for me.

Eagle Thinking

God does not control my choices.

I know that because the Word says it's up to me to "choose this day a blessing or a curse." So I've made up my mind to do whatever I'm able to do each day to make choices that can help the Father's blessing to stay on my life.

I'm also not waiting until everything is all figured out or perfect in my life before I try what I feel God wants me to try. No way! He tells me, and I believe Him that "if I wait for perfect conditions, I will never get anything done."

Therefore I would rather attempt to do something great and fail, than attempt to do nothing and succeed. There's no way I'm going to play it so safe that when my life is just about over I have the horrible regrets of those people in that convalescent hospital.

I refuse to limit myself by my fear to fail. I will not be ruled by a dread that things may not work out. I'm going to take the risks God wants me to take so that I can live my life to the fullest for Him.

If I fail, I fail.

But at least I won't regret that I didn't even try.

I have things I wish with all my heart that I had done differently. But if God could use David and Peter, then He can forgive me and use me. So I won't allow my regrets to stop me from being who He wants me to be. I "flat out" won't do that! And when I fail, because at times I will, I've decided to let God know I'm sincerely sorry and then let Him help me get back up to try again.

I've decided to do whatever it takes to live today, so that God's plan and future for me can actually happen. I'm not even going to talk about my past anymore. That has only made the hurts worse. It only kept reminding me of all the pain.

No wonder the Father doesn't want me doing that! He wants the very best for me as my kind Dad. I'm going to do exactly what He says and forget all that. It's nothing compared to what He wants to do in my life. As my Dad, God is really excited about the brand new thing He's already begun to do. So I'm getting "on board" with looking at my life that way, too.

I won't let the past rob me of my future.

I've said goodbye to my past.

Thinking about it is not "my friend" anymore.

So when thoughts of the past come, I'm determined to refuse them. And I've made up my mind to do all I can to just as swiftly as possible change those negative thoughts to something encouraging and positive.

To forgive is a choice. It's not an emotion.

So I've made the decision to forgive all those who have hurt me. And that settles it. It's over. I'm not going to focus on what they did anymore.

And I'm determined to keep on choosing to forgive, no matter what new hurts may come.

I know that if I hang on to a grudge, my relationship with that person will be poisoned by my bitterness. Then it can never be the same between us. I won't allow that to happen. This means that all the days of my life I will forgive, no matter what people do that is painful for me. I won't allow the hurts from people to rob me of having the healthy, rewarding, relationships that the Father has planned for me to have. He knows how much I need them in my life.

I finally get it!

This journey through life is not just about Jesus and Me.

Because often the bridges over the hard places in life come from the encouragement of those that my kind Father has given me as my friends and family so that we can give strength and courage to one another.

Therefore it's settled!

I won't ever again live my life like a tree alone in the forest, with no one in my life to help me get back up again when I fall down.

I will try things that the Father wants me to try, even if it's not a comfortable stretch.

If I get hurt trying, He will be there to help me, comfort me and give me the courage to try again.

I know I'm going to get hurt living life as an eagle. But I would get hurt if I stayed in the chicken coop where life and God's plan for me can never happen. There's also no one there who is kindred with me because chickens don't think or feel anything like an eagle. They can never understand me. My longings will never make any sense to them at all.

I may "visit" that place once and awhile when life gets hard and I go backwards temporarily during a struggle. But I will get out of there just as fast as possible.

I never want to live there again.

When life is really difficult for me, I'm convinced to the core of who I am that my caring Dad understands how I'm feeling. He will be there for me. He will comfort me.

He will help me get to the other side of any hard time I'm up against.

I've also made up my mind that I'm going to believe what the Father in His Word tells me I am.

It's **His** voice and **His** Word I will listen to. I will **not** listen to the destructive voices of my past, or the condemning accusations of the evil one about my failures. I am keenly aware that **any** listening to them at all will only defeat me and very swiftly.

The Father believes in me and that's what I've passionately decided to hang on to so that I have courage to live the plans that God has for me as my Dad.

Therefore, I will remind myself when I get discouraged:

If God could use an ordinary person like William Seymour, He surely can use me.

If He could use David, I know He can use someone like me who has failed in so many ways.

If He could understand and encourage Gideon when he felt inadequate, He will do that for me whenever I feel insecure.

If He could use an uneducated plumber who couldn't even read, He can definitely use me.

To fully accept how the Father sees me, I've decided to do my part by changing the way I think. I will keep on doing this, no matter what losses and disappointments come my way.

I'm also not going to put Him using me on hold while I wait for something to happen that looks "important" to me or "big" to other people. I've decided to do what God says is the most important thing I can ever do to be used by Him doing all I can to see those each day that my new Dad wants me to love for Him. And I have passionately decided to live and think this way, no matter how small that effort may seem to me.

How totally encouraging it is to know that it's never too late for God to use me. I'm never too old for that to happen! Therefore, I refuse to ever believe that I'm too old to make a difference for God. Instead I'm going to live life to the fullest for Him and as I do, He will keep His promise to "renew my youth like the eagle." To help me stay this determined I will remind myself that this is what He did for Caleb:

> "The Lord has let me live just as He spoke, these forty-five years, from the time that the Lord spoke this word to Moses, when Israel walked in the wilderness. And now, behold, I am eighty-five years old. I am still as strong today as I was in the day Moses sent me. As my strength was then, so my strength is now, for war and for going out and coming in. So give me the Mountain the Lord promised me that day long ago."
>
> Joshua 14:10-12 NASB/NCV

Finally, Jesus said: "The gateway to life is very narrow and the road is difficult. Only a few ever find it." Matthew 7:14 NLT But I've decided that though the road is "narrow" and "difficult," it's worth all the hard choices I have to make so that I can stay on the path to freedom, and never drift away from it again.

When I understood all this, I really had fun revising the ending of "The Eagle and the Chicken Story."

Here it is...

Once there was a man who found an eagle's egg and put it into the nest of a prairie chicken.

The eaglet hatched with the brood of chicks and grew up with them. All of his life the eagle, thinking he was a prairie chicken, did what prairie chickens do.

He scratched in the dirt for seeds and insects to eat. He clucked and cackled. He flew in a brief thrashing of wings and flurry of feathers, no more than a few feet off the ground. After all, that's how prairie chickens were supposed to fly.

Years passed and the eagle grew very old. One day, he saw a magnificent bird far above him in the cloudless sky.

Gliding with graceful majesty on the powerful wind currents, it soared with scarcely a beat of its strong, golden wings.

"What a beautiful bird," said the eagle to his neighbor. "What is it?"

"That's an eagle, the chief of birds," the neighbor clucked. "So don't give it a second thought. You could never be like him."

But something happened!

He saw for the first time who he really was!

He finally realized that the only thing keeping him in the chicken coop was himself.

So he decided to try.

He spread his wings and rose up like an eagle does. As he did, he left behind the place he had been stuck all his life.

Soon he experienced a kindred closeness with other eagles who shared his same longings.

Finding them gave him a new courage during the hard times.

Walking closely with them helped him to not give up thinking like an eagle, no matter what it would take to do that and no matter how discouraging life can still be at times.

There were still hardships and hurts to press through.

But it was worth it all because finally he was who he was always meant to be.

Being free was scary at times. Yet he knew he would never go back. He had felt lost most of his life. Now he felt like he had come back home to where he belonged.

Sometimes he did look back at where he used to live.

During those moments, it saddened him that it took him so long to leave that place where he felt so empty and alone.

Then in the next breath, the sadness always became a stunning burst of life as he celebrated that he didn't live there anymore.

***

As this book is ending and you continue on with your Journey in life, I want to be vulnerably honest with you.

I wish I had seen what's in "Revival on the Horizon" when I was much younger. That's why sharing it with you means so much to me.

It's my heritage I'm passing on to anyone who reads it.

If it helps you to find your way a whole lot sooner than I did, I'm overwhelmingly grateful because God longs for each of His sons and daughters to experience the fullness of His plan for them, and He wants them to find their way there as young as possible.

These are His fatherly words to spur us on in this challenging, but rewarding adventure of living for Him.

"My dear child. I fully understand that 'hope deferred makes the heart sick.'

But the good news is that when dreams come true, there is much joy.' And I *do* have a dream, a vision and a wondrous plan for you.

I also am passionate about doing all I can to help you find your way there so that you can fulfill all I've planned for you.

I will do this because of My love for you.

But also because I need you to be part of My coming again with the fire of My Revival.

I need you, just like I needed those simple, ordinary people who were in an upper room after My Son left them and returned home to Me. When they walked out of that room, they were never the same. They had been indelibly changed by their encounter with Me.

From that day My presence was strong upon them. They began to love like My Son gave His very life to teach them.

Even when it meant they could not do everything they personally wanted to do, they united with other believers.

These ordinary women and men, and the young people who were with them as time went on, turned the world upside down.

There weren't even many of them to start with.

Yet the fire of Revival spread through them because they had so much love for anyone I asked them to care about for Me.

This is also My destiny for you."

- Your Father

SOURCES

Quotations marked (Frank Bartleman) are taken from Azusa Street. Copyright © 1980 by Logos International. Used by permission. All rights reserved.

Quotations marked (Webster's New Collegiate Dictionary) are taken from the Webster's New Collegiate Dictionary. Copyright © 1981 by G. & C. Merriam Co. Used by permission. All rights reserved.

Scripture quotations marked (KJV) are taken from the King James Version. Copyright © 1975 by Thomas Nelson, Inc. Used by permission. All rights reserved.

Scripture quotations marked (NLT) are taken from the Holy Bible, New Living Translation. Copyright © 1996. Used by permission of Tyndale House Publishers, Inc. All rights reserved.

Scripture References marked (NASB) are taken from the New American Standard Bible, © 1960, 1963, 1968, 1971, 1972, 1973, 1975, 1977 by The Lockman Foundation. Used by permission.

Scripture quotations marked (NIV) are taken from The Holy Bible, New International Version. Copyright © 1973, 1978, 1984 by International Bible Society. Used by permission of Zondervan Publishing House. All rights reserved.

Scripture quotations marked (AMPLIFIED) are taken from The AMPLIFIED Bible. Copyright © 1965 by Zondervan Publishing House. Used by permission. All rights reserved.

Scripture quotations marked (MOFFATT) are taken from The Bible, James MOFFATT Translation. Copyright © 1950, 1952, 1953, 1954 by James A. R. MOFFATT. Harper & Row Publishers. Used by permission. All rights reserved.

Scripture quotations marked (NCV) are taken from the Holy Bible, New Century Translation. Copyright © 1987, 1988, 1991, 1995 Used by permission of Word Publishing, Inc. All rights reserved.

ANOTHER BOOK BY THE AUTHOR

THE TRIP TO FREEDOM

This book captures how Ruth learned to walk through the door to freedom using God's Word, after 45 years of horrific abuse.

She writes with such a vulnerable honesty and shares the Word in such a deeply personal way that since it was first published in 1998, countless people from across the nations have found their own path to freedom through reading it. Miraculous healings have happened in places of devastating emotional pain that they had felt were impossible. Young and old experience the Father as a kind, loving Dad. For many it's an encounter with the first real Father they've ever known.

Singles of all ages seriously need to read "The Trip to Freedom."

This book will help you know if a person you are getting involved with is a mistake, or if the relationship has the potential to be a healthy one. That's why reading it can protect any single, including the younger generation who are at the beginning of their journey of discovering who they want to date, from the suffering Ruth experienced due to her learning all this about relationships the hard way.

ABOUT THE MINISTRY

OUR VISION

Reaching across Generations, Denominations, Regions, and Nations to those with a yearning for Revival Fire to visit God's people again.

Helping a Fatherless Younger Generation know God as a loving Dad.

Imparting to people a Prophetic Message of Hope and Encouragement to help them have the courage to live the Father's Purpose for them.

Restoring the Love and Unity that ignited in the Book of Acts Revival, setting the world on fire.

Inspiring intimate worship in the Holy of Holies, including imparting a Prophetic Ministry on the Harp through Ruth as a Davidic Psalmist

TO CONTACT THE MINISTRY

If you are interested in getting more information about who we are and what we do, please visit us online at www.lighthouse-of-hope.org. Also if you would like to inquire about having Ruth and Barry come to your group to minister, please send an email to ruth@lighthouse-of-hope.org or barry@lighthouse-of-hope.org, or call us at 425-775-3904.

www.lighwww.lighthouse-of-hope.org

facebook.com/LighthouseOfHopeMinistries